popknitting

BOLD MOTIFS USING COLOR & STITCH

BRITT-MARIE CHRISTOFFERSSON

Translation by Carol Huebscher Rhoades

INTERWEAVE.
interweave.com

TRANSLATION: Carol Huebscher Rhoades

TECHNICAL EDITING: Kate Atherley

DESIGN: Lora Lamm

PHOTOGRAPHY: Thomas Harrysson (unless otherwise specified)

ILLUSTRATIONS: Katarina Widegren

PRODUCTION: Katherine Jackson

First published in 2009 by Hemslöjdens förlag – Handcraft Publishers
Association of Swedish Handcraft Organizations (SHR)
www.hemslojdensforlag.se

Interweave Press LLC
201 East Fourth Street
Loveland, CO 80537-5655 USA
interweave.com

Printed in China by C&C Offset

Library of Congress Cataloging-in-Publication Data

Christoffersson, Britt-Marie.
 [Stickning. English]
 Pop knitting : bold motifs using color & stitch / Britt-Marie Christoffersson ;
translated by Carol Huebscher Rhoades.
    p. cm.
 ISBN 978-1-59668-782-0 (pbk.)
 1. Sweaters. 2. Knitting--Patterns. 3. Needlework--Patterns. 4. Color in design. I. Title.
 TT825.C42312913 2012
 746.43'20432--dc23
                    2012001361

10 9 8 7 6 5 4 3 2 1

CONTENTS

FOREWORD

With *Pop Knitting: Bold Motifs Using Color & Stitch*, I want to show how knitting has the potential for endless variety. I want to inspire you and every knitter to try new patterns, and I hope that my ideas will, in turn, lead you to new ideas for your knitting.

My interest in handknitting came early on. When I was a child, I always liked to have something to do with my hands. I think that the more handwork becomes ingrained in our lives, the more meaningful art from our hands will become. Added to this is my fascination with the colors and shapes that build patterns.

I generally use 2-ply wool yarns for my knitting. I often blend yarns from different companies to get the color results I want. I usually prefer a firm knit fabric and most often knit on U.S. size 1.5 (2.5 mm) needles at a gauge of about 28–30 sts in 4" (10 cm).

The patterns in this book are presented in groups with a short presentation of each group's technique and my thoughts about it. Some are already well-known patterns that one can find in other knitting books; the rest are my own designs. My experience has been that, when knitting to learn a technique, ideas about other pattern constructions arise.

I haven't included any instructions for finished garments as you can easily find them in other inspiring resources.

Today there are a large number of old and new books that deal with handknitting from all points of view. Most of the books are only available now in libraries. I recommend studying these if you have questions that my book doesn't answer.

Britt-Marie Christoffersson
Halmstad, Sweden, March 2009

PATTERNS

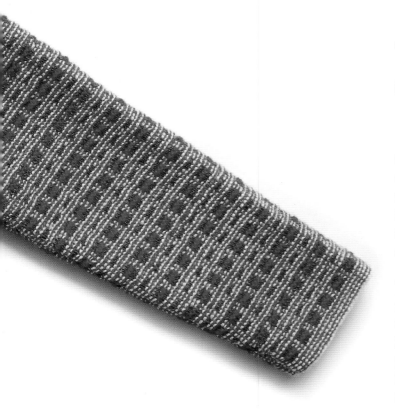

TWO-COLOR GARTER STITCH, FOUR ROWS

When you change colors in garter stitch, what I would call "color blending" occurs on the wrong-side rows. Most often it's not the look you want, but I've used that effect to get a garter stitch structure with two different colors.

Two-color garter stitch is worked with double-pointed needles or a circular. The knitting is turned on every other row, after you've first knitted a right-side row with color 1 and purled a wrong-side row with color 2. The following two rows are purled with color 1 and knit with color 2.

This cardigan is created from the pattern Two-color Garter Stitch, Four Rows #4 (see page 18). Use a pattern for a plain stockinette stitch cardigan and simply work the pieces in the pattern stitch. No further adjustment is needed. This sample has an unshaped body and a set-in sleeve on a shaped armhole with a simple crew neck. Stitches are picked up around the neckline and a single garter ridge is worked in one of the pattern colors.

Two-Color Garter Stitch, Four Rows # 1

Stitch count: any number.
Two colors.
The pattern looks like garter stitch but has purl rows.
Use double-pointed needles or circular.
CO with color 1.

ROW 1 (RS): With color 2, knit. Do not turn.

ROW 2 (RS): With color 1, purl. Turn.

ROW 3 (WS): With color 2, purl. Do not turn.

ROW 4 (WS): With color 1, knit. Turn.

Repeat Rows 1–4.

Adding in a third color can create very different fabrics.

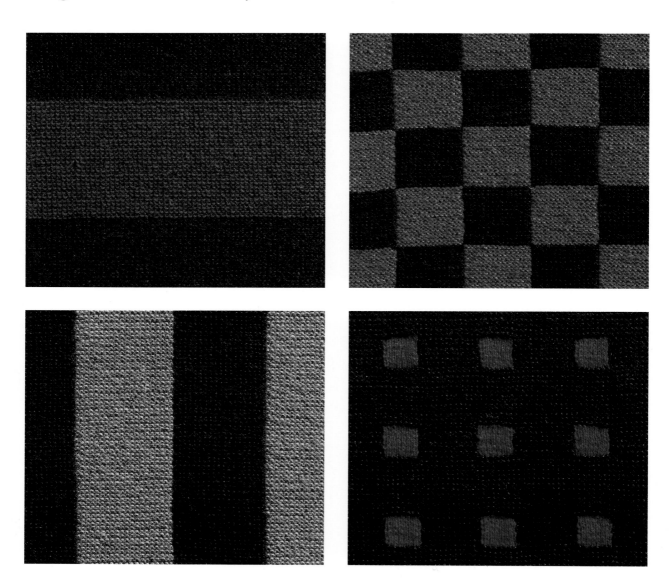

TOP LEFT: After a few repeats of the pattern, change the yarn used for color 1.

TOP RIGHT: Use the intarsia method (see page 207) to create vertical stripes. Keep color 1 consistent across the rows but alternate two different yarns for color 2. After a few repeats, swap the positions of the two different color 2 yarns.

BOTTOM LEFT: Use the intarsia method to create vertical stripes. Keep color 1 consistent across the rows but alternate two different yarns for color 2. Change the look even more by changing yarns for color 1 when you change for color 2.

BOTTOM RIGHT: Work patches of stockinette stitch in a third color at regular intervals in the fabric.

Use these garter stitch fabrics in combination with other fabrics for different effects.

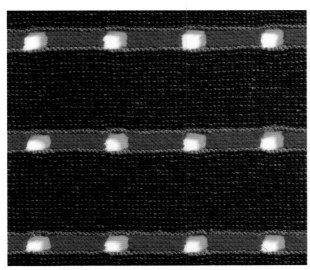

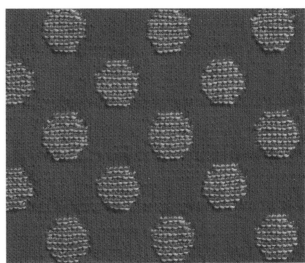

TOP LEFT: This swatch features intarsia patches of Two-color Garter Stitch, Four Rows #1 (see page 10) against a stockinette stitch background.

TOP RIGHT: Using the intarsia method (see page 207), work vertical stripes of two different garter stitch fabrics. In this swatch, the stripes alternate Two-color Garter Stitch, Four Rows #1 and standard garter stitch worked with two-row stripes.

BOTTOM LEFT: In this swatch, a single ridge of a contrasting color is worked above and below garter stitch strips worked in a fourth color.

BOTTOM RIGHT: This swatch is a relatively simple but clever variation of Two-color Garter Stitch, Four Rows #2 (see page 14): change the position of the stockinette stitch stripes and the garter stitch patches. Create dots by starting with 5 stitches in the garter stitch fabric, adding 1 either side per ridge until you have 9 stitches. Work three ridges at the full width, and reduce the stitches again, 1 per side per ridge, until you have 5 again.

Two-Color Garter Stitch, Four Rows #2

Stitch count: multiple of 13.
Two colors.
Use double-pointed needles or circular.
CO with color 1.

ROW 1 (WS): *With color 1, p3. With color 2, k7. With color 1, p3; rep from *.

ROW 2 (RS): With color 1, knit across.

ROW 3 (WS): *With color 1, p3, sl 7 wyf, p3; rep from *.

ROW 4 (RS): *With color 2, sl 3 wyb, p7, sl 3 wyb; rep from *. Do not turn.

ROW 5 (RS): With color 1, knit across.

Repeat Rows 1–5.

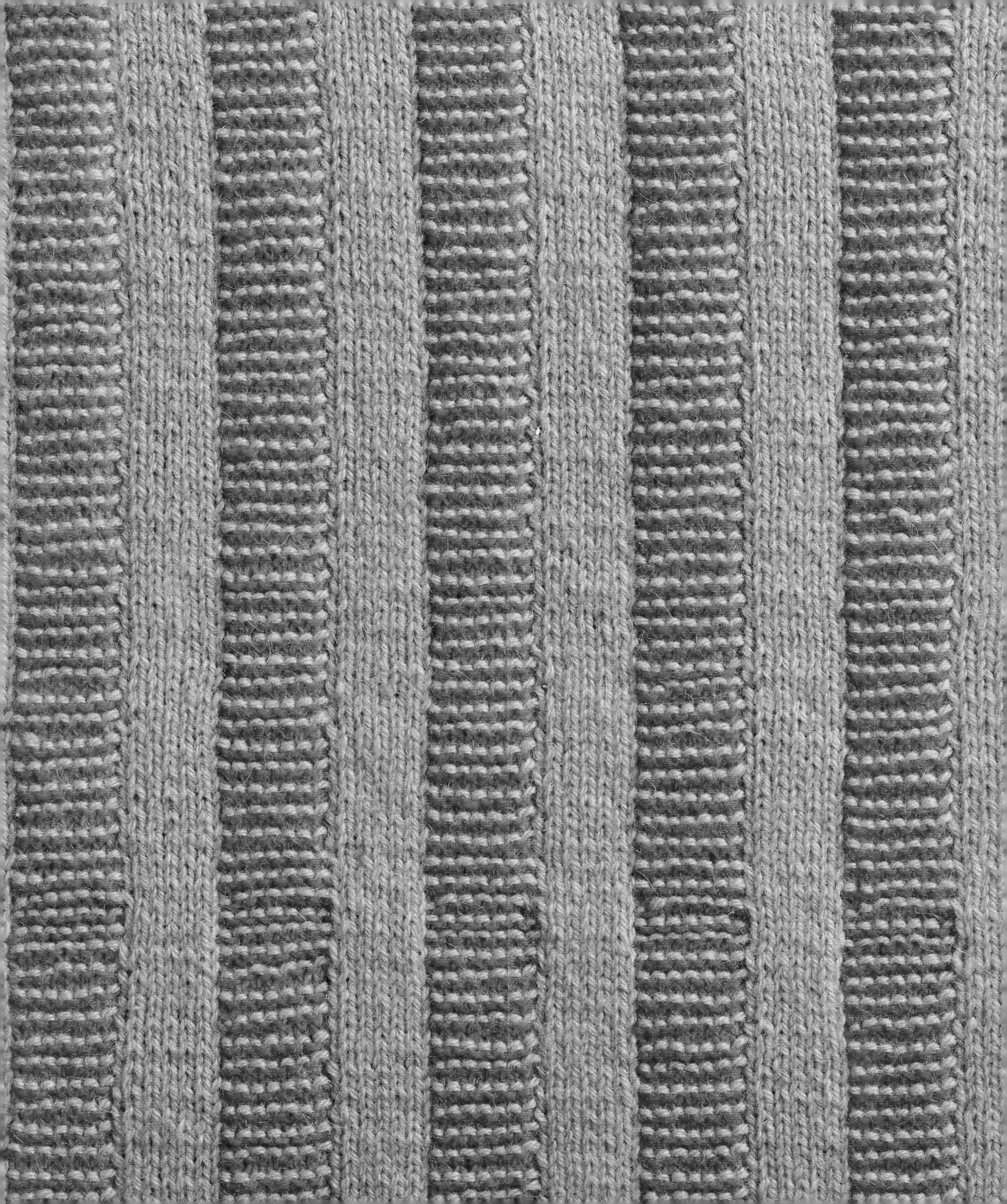

Two-Color Garter Stitch, Four Rows #3

Each block has 10 sts.
Each block uses a separate strand of yarn.
For information about intarsia, see the Techniques section (page 207).
These instructions are for a two-color block.
CO with color 1.

ROW 1 (WS): With color 1, purl.

ROW 2 (RS): With color 1, knit.

ROW 3 (WS): With color 1, purl.

ROW 4 (RS): *With color 1, k2. With color 2, p6. With color 1, k2; rep from *.

ROW 5 (WS): With color 1, purl.

ROW 6 (RS): *With color 1, k2, sl 6 wyb, k2; rep from *.

ROW 7 (WS): *With color 1, p2. With color 2, k6. With color 1, p2; rep from *.

ROW 8 (RS): With color 1, knit.

ROW 9 (WS): *With color 1, p2, sl 6 wyf, p2; rep from *.

ROW 10 (RS): *With color 1, k2. With color 2, p6. With color 1, k2; rep from *.

ROW 11 (WS): With color 1, purl.

ROW 12 (RS): *With color 1, k2, sl 6 wyb, k2; rep from *.

ROW 13 (WS): *With color 1, p2. With color 2, k6. With color 1, p2; rep from *.

ROW 14 (RS): With color 1, knit.

ROW 15 (WS): With color 1, purl.

ROW 16 (RS): With color 1, knit.

Change to two new colors and repeat Rows 1–6.

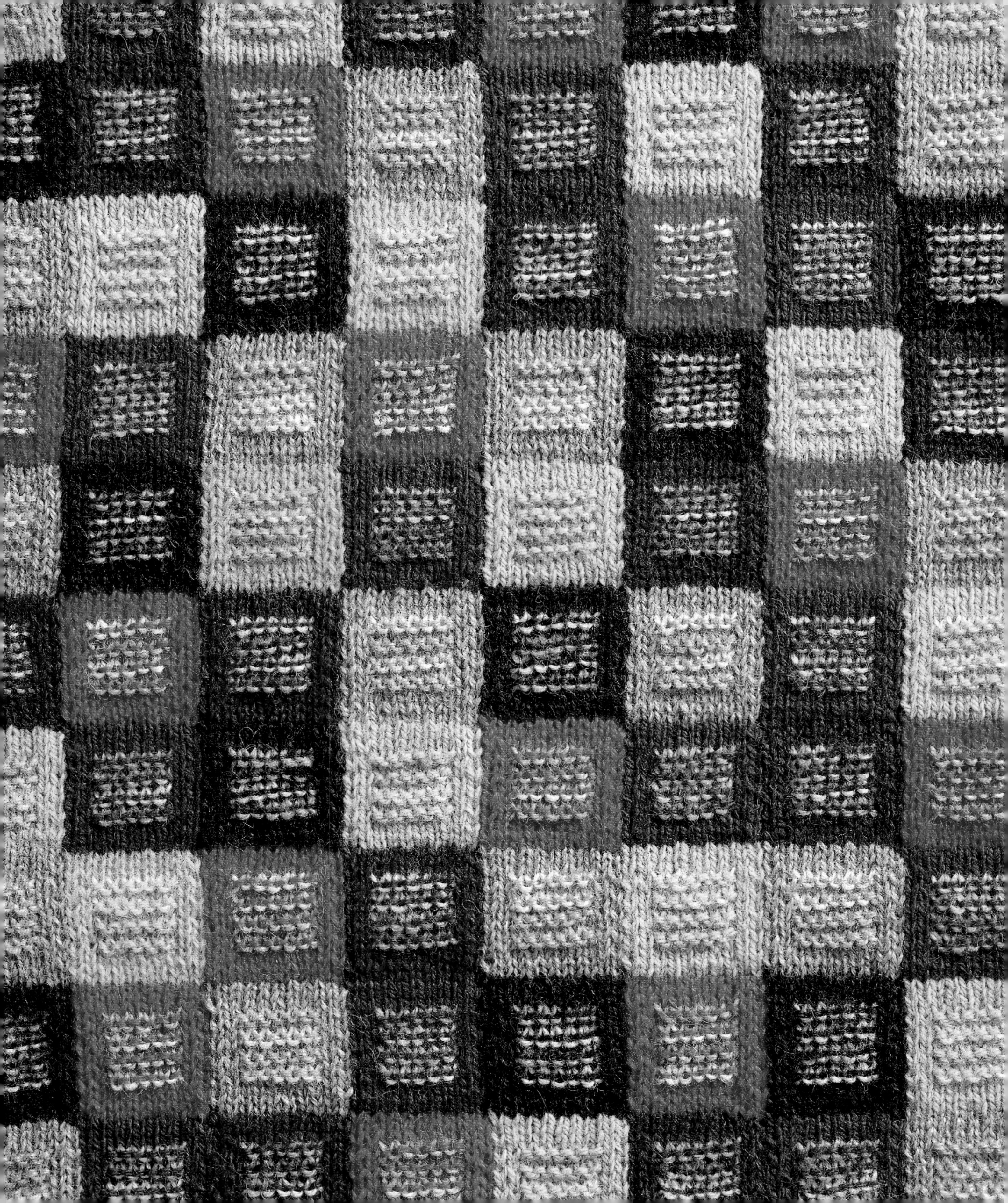

Two-Color Garter Stitch, Four Rows #4

Stitch count: multiple of 5.
Three colors.
Use double-pointed needles or circular.
CO with color 1.

ROW 1 (WS): With color 2, knit. Do not turn.

ROW 2 (WS): With color 1, purl. Turn.

ROW 3 (RS): With color 2, purl. Do not turn.

ROW 4 (RS): *With color 1, k1. With color 3, k3. With color 1, k1; rep from *. Turn.

ROW 5 (WS): *With color 2, k1, p3, k1; rep from *. Do not turn.

ROW 6 (WS): *With color 1, p1, sl 3 wyf, p1; rep from *. Turn.

ROW 7 (RS): With color 2, purl. Turn.

ROW 8 (WS): *With color 3, sl 1 wyf, p3, sl 1 wyf; rep from *. Turn.

ROW 9 (RS): With color 1, knit. Turn.

Repeat Rows 1–9.

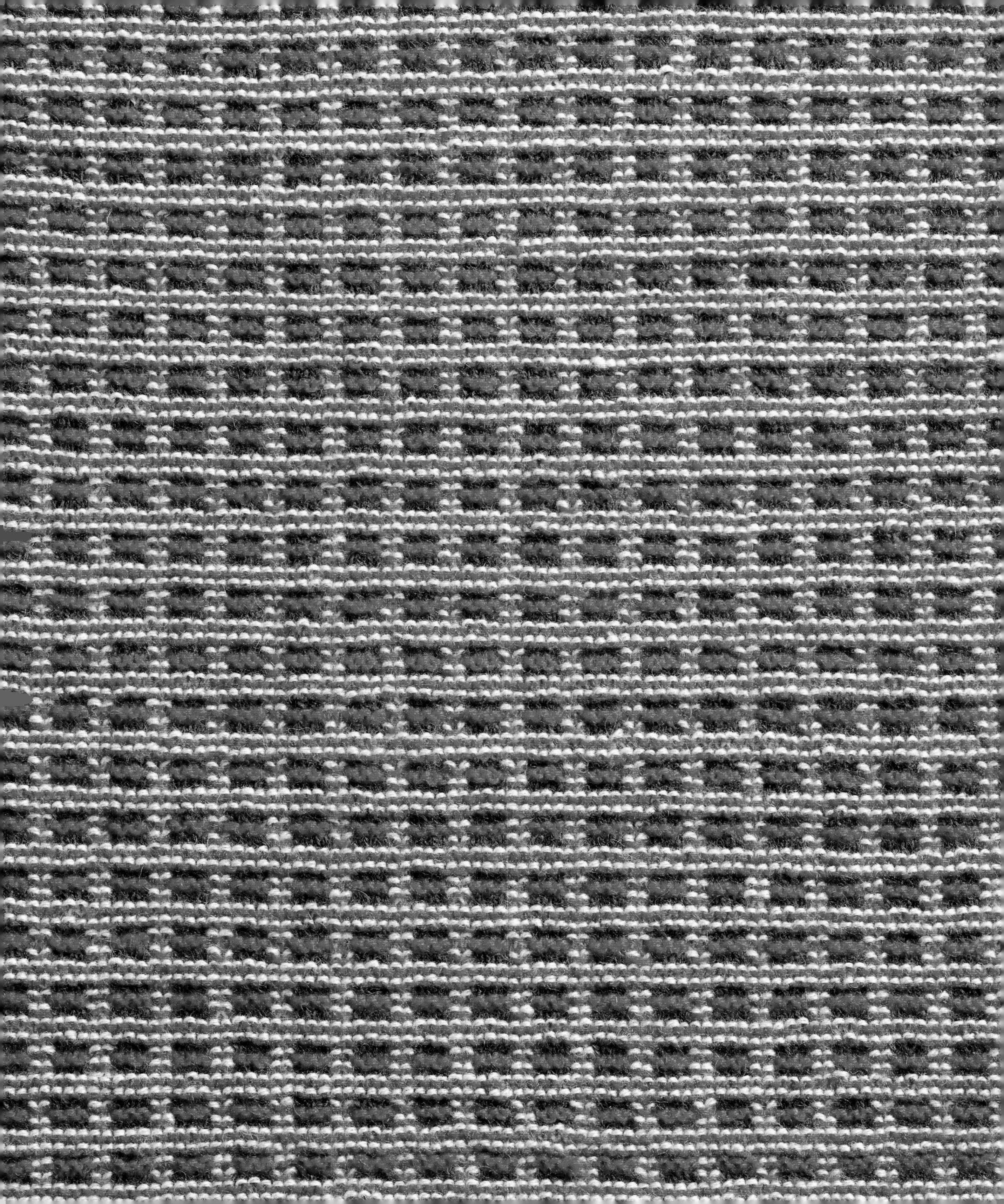

TWO-COLOR GARTER STITCH, THREE ROWS

Two-color garter stitch patterns with no color blending on the right side are knit with double-pointed needles or a circular. For this technique, the repeat is three rows: on the right side, you work a knit and then a purl row with color 1 followed by a knit row with color 2.

This cardigan is created from the pattern Two-color Garter Stitch, Three Rows #2 (see page 26). This sample has an unshaped body and drop sleeve with a simple crew neck following the garment template given on pages 208–209. The cuff and body edgings are worked using the pattern shown on page 24. Stitches are picked up around the neckline and a facing is worked so that when turned in and sewn down on the inside of the garment, the stockinette side shows.

Two-color Garter Stitch, Three Rows #1

Stitch count: multiple of 8.
Three colors.
Use double-pointed needles or circular.
CO with color 1.

ROW 1 (WS): With color 1, knit. Turn.

ROW 2 (RS): With color 2, knit. Do not turn.

ROW 3 (RS): With color 1, knit. Turn.

ROW 4 (WS): With color 1, knit. Do not turn.

ROW 5 (WS): With color 2, purl. Turn.

ROW 6 (RS): With color 1, knit. Turn.

Work Rows 1–5 once more.

ROW 12 (RS): *With color 1, k2. With color 3, k4. With color 1, k2; rep from *. Turn.

ROW 13(WS): Work as for Row 11. Turn.

ROW 14 (RS): With color 2, knit. Do not turn.

ROW 15 (RS): With color 1, knit. Turn.

ROW 16 (WS): With color 1, knit. Do not turn.

ROW 17 (WS): With color 2, purl. Turn.

ROW 18 (RS): With color 1, knit. Turn.

Repeat Rows 1–8.

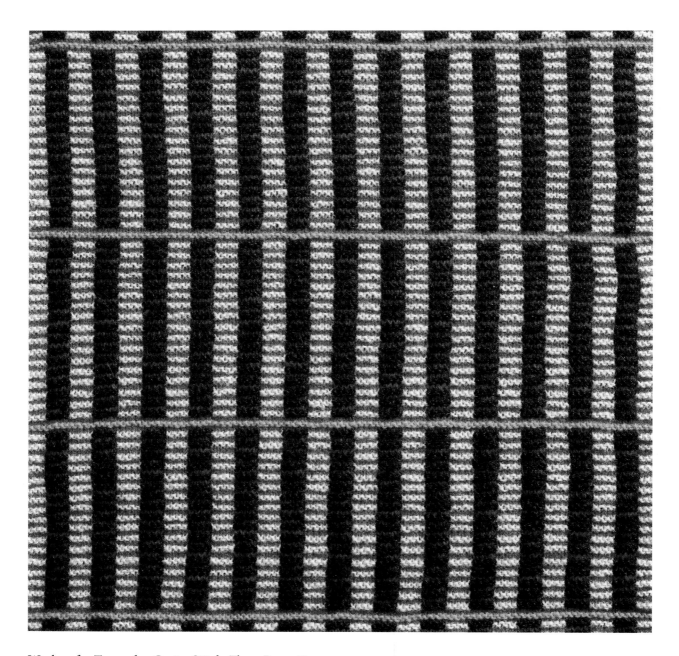

Work as for Two-color Garter Stitch, Three Rows #1
(see page 22) with three colors, but eliminate the plain
ridges between the two-color ridges. Use a fourth color
to create a contrasting color ridge between repeats of
two-color ridges.

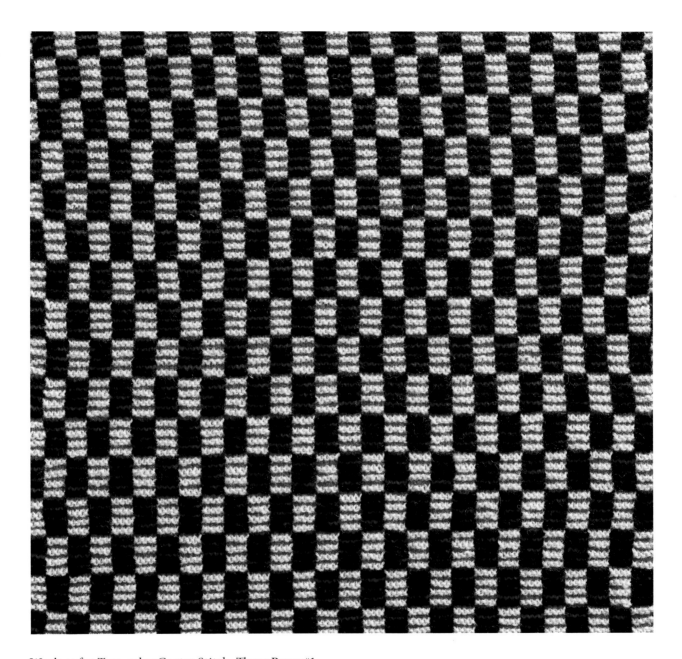

Work as for Two-color Garter Stitch, Three Rows #1 (see page 22) with three colors, but eliminate the plain ridges between the two-color ridges. After four ridges, alternate the positions of the blocks to create a check effect.

Two-color Garter Stitch, Three Rows #2

Stitch count: multiple of 8.
Three colors
Use double-pointed needles or circular.
CO with color 3.

ROW 1 (WS): With color 3, purl. Turn.

ROW 2 (RS): *With color 1, k1. With color 2, k7; rep from *. Turn.

ROW 3 (WS): *With color 2, k7. With color 1, k1; rep from *. Turn.

ROW 4 (RS): With color 3, knit. Do not turn.

ROW 5 (RS): *With color 1, k2. With color 2, k5. With color 1, k1; rep from *. Turn.

ROW 6 (WS): *With color 1, k1. With color 2, k5. With color 1, k2; rep from *. Do not turn.

ROW 7 (WS): With color 3, purl. Turn.

ROW 8 (RS): *With color 1, k3. With color 2, k3. With color 1, k2; rep from *. Turn.

ROW 9 (WS): *With color 1, k2. With color 2, k3. With color 1, k3; rep from *. Turn.

ROW 10 (RS): With color 3, knit. Do not turn.

ROW 11 (RS): *With color 1, k4. With color 2, k1. With color 1, k3; rep from *. Turn.

ROW 12 (WS): *With color 1, k3. With color 2, k1. With color 1, k4; rep from *. Do not turn.

ROW 13 (WS): With color 3, purl. Turn.

ROW 14 (RS): *With color 2, k4. With color 1, k1. With color 2, k3; rep from *. Turn.

ROW 15 (WS): *With color 2, k3. With color 1, k1. With color 2, k4; rep from *. Turn.

ROW 16 (RS): With color 3, knit. Do not turn.

ROW 17 (RS): *With color 2, k3. With color 1, k3. With color 2, k2; rep from *. Turn.

ROW 18 (WS): *With color 2, k2. With color 1, k3. With color 2, k3; rep from *. Do not turn.

ROW 19 (WS): With color 3, purl. Turn.

ROW 20 (RS): *With color 2, k2. With color 1, k5. With color 2, k1; rep from *. Turn.

ROW 21 (WS): *With color 2, k1. With color 1, k5. With color 2, k2; rep from *. Turn.

ROW 22 (RS): With color 3, knit. Do not turn.

ROW 23 (RS): *With color 2, k1. With color 1, k7; rep from *. Turn.

ROW 24 (WS): *With color 1, k7. With color 2, k1; rep from *. Do not turn.

Repeat Rows 1–24.

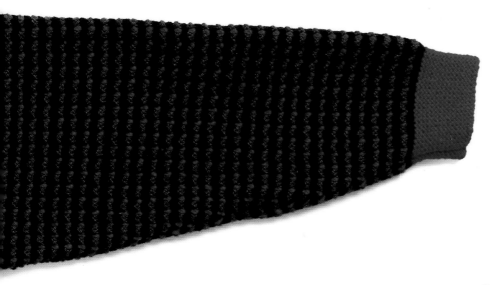

APRON DESIGNS

There are some designs I love that I call "un-designed." They can be found on old hand towels and dishrags—the simple striped and checked cotton fabrics that were once woven in small Swedish weaving studios. These printed patterns also rekindle memories, reminding me of the aprons worn by my mother's generation. They have inspired me to knit these check patterns.

This cardigan is created from another simple check pattern variation. Two rows of stockinette are worked in blue and then a single garter stitch ridge is worked, alternating 2 stitches in green and 1 stitch in red. This sample has an unshaped body and drop sleeve with a simple crew neck following the garment template given on pages 208–209. The cuff and body edgings are worked in garter stitch. Stitches are picked up around the neckline and a facing is worked so that when turned in and sewn down on the inside of the garment, the stockinette side shows.

Variations of a basic check pattern using two colors. Using a lighter color for the foreground puts the emphasis on the grid lines. Two rows are worked in the foreground color, and two rows are worked alternating between the foreground and the background colors.

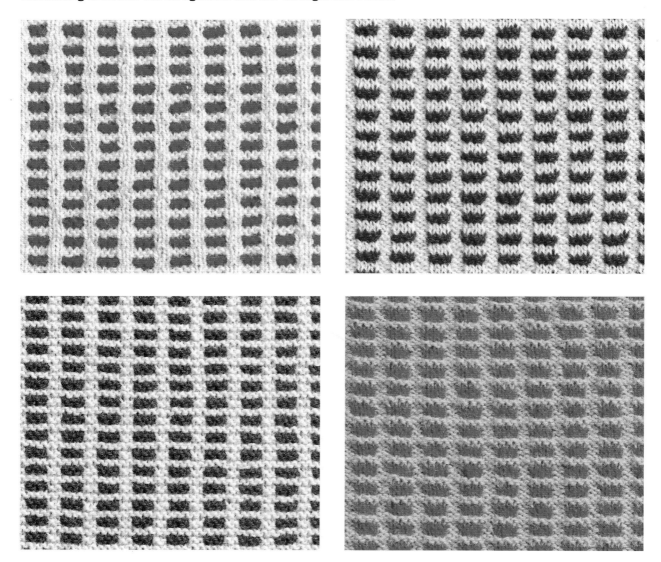

TOP LEFT: Alternate vertical stripes of stockinette stitch in white and vertical stripes of garter stitch ridges alternating between red and white.

TOP RIGHT: Alternate vertical stripes of reverse stockinette stitch in white and vertical stripes of stockinette stitch in two-row stripes of blue and white.

BOTTOM LEFT: Alternate vertical stripes of garter stitch in white and vertical stripes of garter stitch ridges alternating between green and white.

BOTTOM RIGHT: Alternate vertical stripes of reverse stockinette stitch in yellow and vertical stripes alternating a garter ridge in yellow and two rows of stockinette stitch in red.

Variations of a basic check pattern using three or four colors. Two rows are worked in one pair of colors, and two rows are worked in another pair of colors.

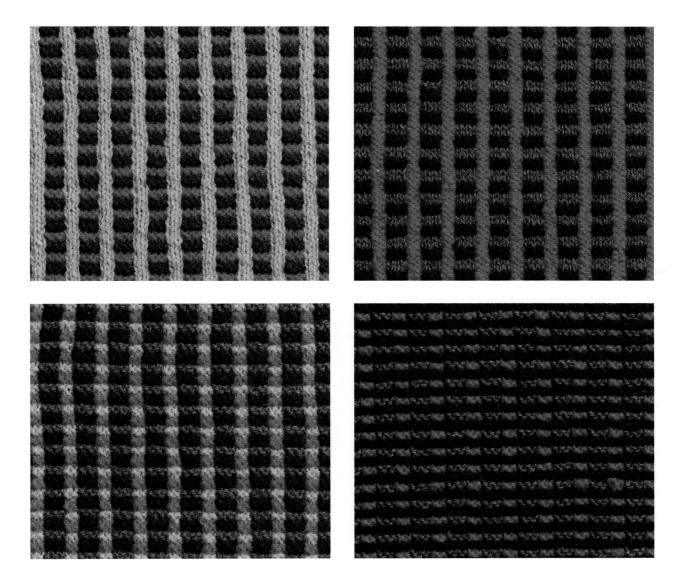

TOP LEFT: Alternate vertical stripes of stockinette stitch in yellow and vertical stripes of garter stitch ridges alternating between red and blue.

TOP RIGHT: Alternate vertical stripes of reverse stockinette stitch in red and vertical stripes alternating a garter ridge in blue and two rows of stockinette stitch in green.

BOTTOM LEFT: Work 2-stitch vertical stripes of garter stitch ridges alternating between yellow and red and 3-stitch vertical stripes of garter stitch ridges alternating between green and blue.

BOTTOM RIGHT: Work two rows in blue and work two rows alternating 2 stitches each in red and green. This gives vertical stripes of garter stitch ridges alternating between blue and red between vertical stripes of garter stitch ridges alternating between blue and green.

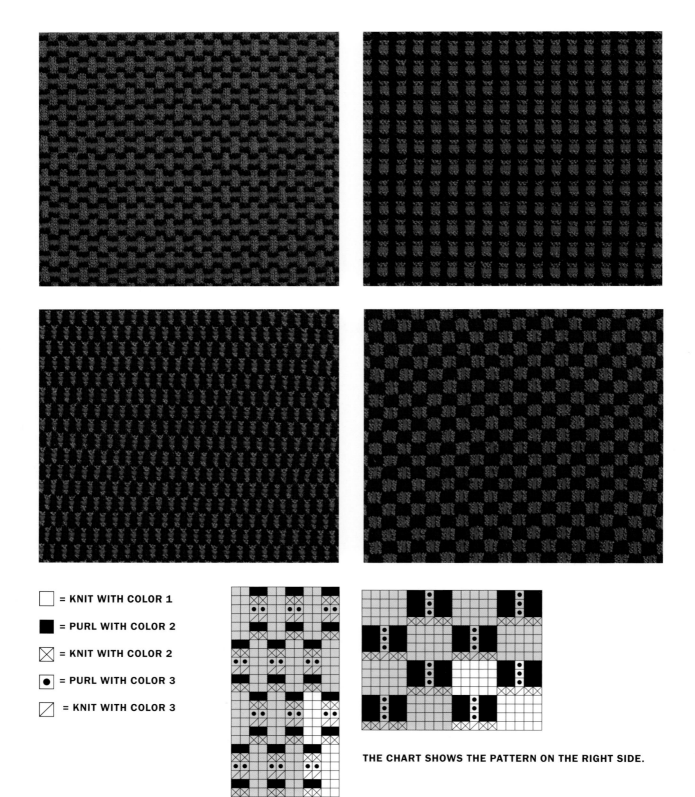

= KNIT WITH COLOR 1

= PURL WITH COLOR 2

= KNIT WITH COLOR 2

= PURL WITH COLOR 3

= KNIT WITH COLOR 3

THE CHART SHOWS THE PATTERN ON THE RIGHT SIDE.

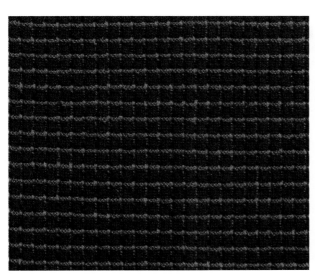

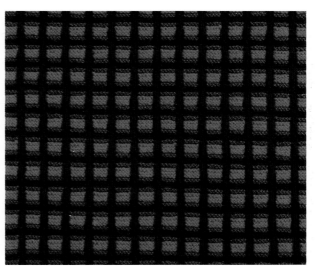

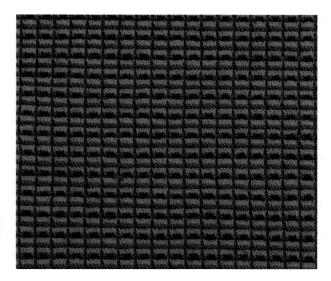

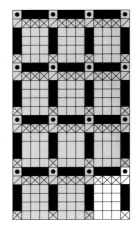

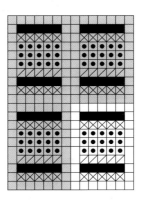

Add in more colors to create more intricate and varied looks.

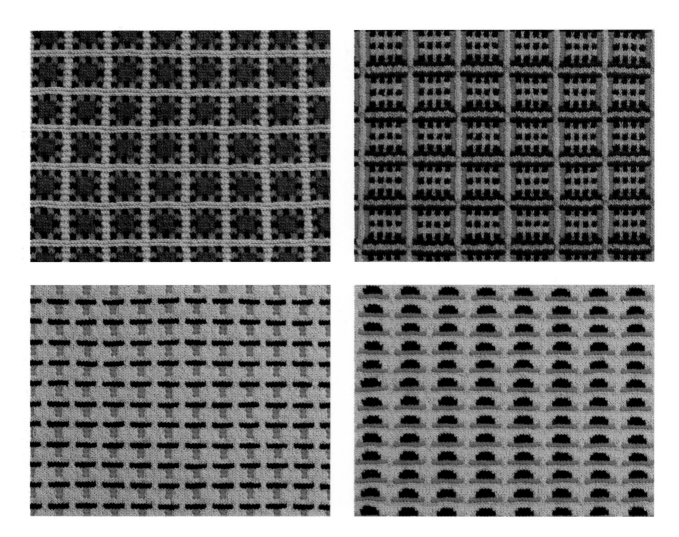

TOP LEFT: Two garter stitch ridges and 2-stitch garter columns frame three-color checks worked in red, blue, and green. The upper and lower portions of the three-color checks are worked by alternating 2 stitches each in red and blue. The center six rows of the check are worked with 2 stitches in red or blue, six in green, and two in red or blue as set.

TOP RIGHT: Blocks of yellow and blue checks are framed by single-stitch garter stitch columns in red and 2-stitch columns of stockinette stitch in yellow. The blue stitches in the block are worked as purls on the RS for further contrast. Between the checks, there are stripes of garter stitch that are worked in green, maintaining the yellow columns, and stripes of alternating 2-stitch blocks of yellow and turquoise.

BOTTOM LEFT: A simpler-to-work fabric is created by working two rows of stockinette stitch alternating black and yellow and four rows alternating stockinette stitch in yellow and garter stitch in red, with two rows of yellow only between the motifs.

BOTTOM RIGHT: A simple variation on the swatch to the left. Two rows alternating between stockinette stitch in yellow and garter stitch in red, follow by four rows in stockinette stitch alternating between black and yellow and four plain rows in yellow. The black patch is shaped by working 2 stitches fewer in black on the final row.

Further combinations change the look even more.

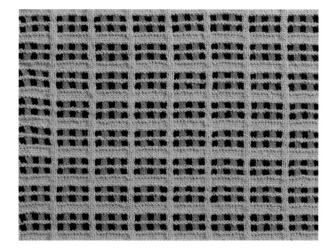

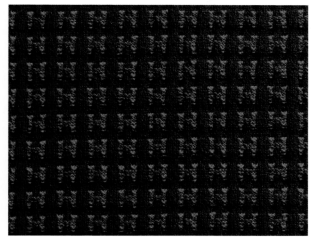

TOP LEFT: Two-row blocks alternating 2 stitches of red and blue are framed by vertical and horizontal stripes of yellow stockinette. Horizontal ridges of garter stitch in yellow provide further definition.

TOP RIGHT: A deceptively simple pattern: four rows of stockinette stitch in blue divide up three-color checks with color changes made on the WS. The upper and lower three rows of the checks are worked by working a pattern of 4 stitches in stockinette stitch in blue, 1 stitch in garter in red, 2 in stockinette stitch in blue and 1 in garter stitch in red. The center three rows of the block are worked by alternating 4 stitches in stockinette stitch in blue and 4 stitches in garter stitch in green.

BOTTOM: On a background of stockinette stitch in yellow, a window design is worked in three contrasting colors. The bottom of the window is created by working 10 stitches in reverse stockinette stitch in red alternating with 2 stitches of stockinette stitch in yellow. The upper portion of the window is worked with a single stitch/single row frame of garter in turquoise and a semicircle shape worked in stockinette stitch in black.

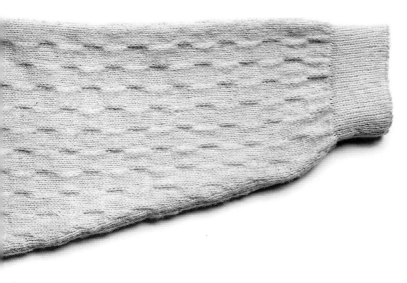

SLIPPED STITCHES AND STOCKINETTE

This technique is a subtle form of patterning because the shadow only shows as you "read" it. The stitches are slipped on every other row, and when the yarn floats on the wrong side, it enlarges the slipped stitch. The stitch is lifted a bit even if you don't tighten the floats. The technique is limited because rounded shapes and the displacement of the pattern over occasional stitches do not show up well.

This cardigan is worked in a 6-stitch, twelve-row variation of the pattern show on the top right of page 41. Use a pattern for a plain stockinette stitch cardigan and simply work the pieces in the pattern stitch. No further adjustment is needed. This sample has an unshaped body and a raglan sleeve shaping with a simple crew neck.

Slipped Stitches and Stockinette #1

Stitch count: multiple of 4.

ROW 1 (WS): Purl.

ROW 2 (RS): *K1, sl 2 wyb, k1; rep from *.

Repeat Rows 1–2.

Changing the number of slipped stitches or the number of stitches worked between the slipped stitches can change the fabric quite radically.

TOP LEFT: Two slipped stitches, 1 knit stitch.

TOP RIGHT: Four slipped stitches, 2 knit stitches.

BOTTOM LEFT: Four slipped stitches, 4 knit stitches.

BOTTOM RIGHT: Five slipped stitches, 1 knit stitch.

Alternate the position of the slipped stitches with the stockinette stitches to create blocks.

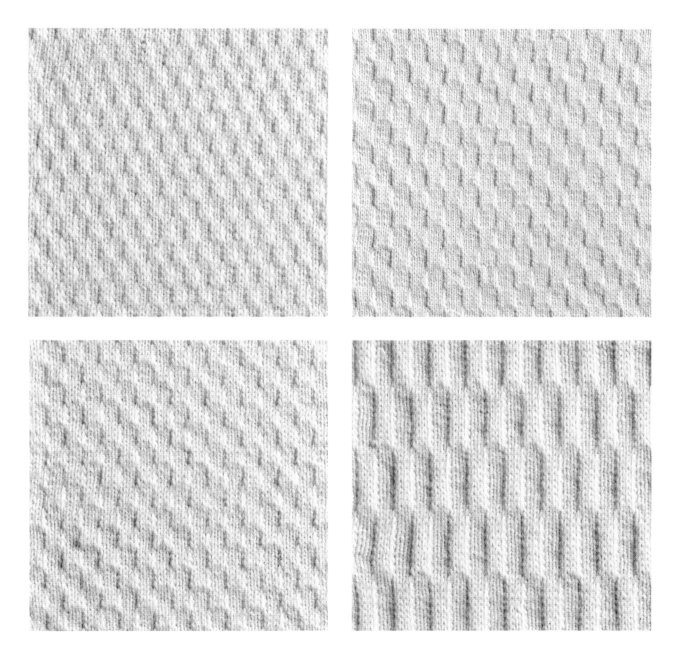

TOP LEFT: Two slipped stitches, 2 knit stitches; alternate their positions every eight rows.

TOP RIGHT: Four slipped stitches, 4 knit stitches; alternate their positions every eight rows.

BOTTOM LEFT: Four slipped stitches, 4 knit stitches; alternate their positions every six rows.

BOTTOM RIGHT: Four slipped stitches, 4 knit stitches; alternate their positions every twenty rows.

Slipped Stitches and Stockinette #2

Stitch count: multiple of 12.

ROW 1 AND ALL ODD-NUMBERED ROWS (WS): Purl.

ROWS 2, 4, 6, 8, AND 10 (RS): *K3, sl 6 wyb, k3; rep from *.

ROWS 12, 14, 16, 18, AND 20 (RS): *Sl 3 wyb, k6, sl 3 wyb; rep from *.

Repeat Rows 1–20.

Slipped Stitches and Stockinette #3

Stitch count: multiple of 8.

ROW 1 AND ALL ODD-NUMBERED ROWS (WS): Purl.

ROWS 2 AND 4 (RS): *K1, sl 7 wyb; rep from *.

ROWS 6 AND 8 (RS): *K2, sl 5 wyb, k1; rep from *.

ROWS 10 AND 12 (RS): *K3, sl 3 wyb, k3; rep from *.

ROW 14 (RS): *K4, sl 1 wyb, k3; rep from *.

ROWS 16 AND 18 (RS): *Sl 4 wyb, k1, sl 3 wyb; rep from *.

ROWS 20 AND 22 (RS): *Sl 3 wyb, k3, sl 2 wyb; rep from *.

ROWS 24 AND 26 (RS): *Sl 2 wyb, k5, sl 1 wyb; rep from *.

ROW 28 (RS): *Sl 1 wyb, k7; rep from *.

Repeat Rows 1–28.

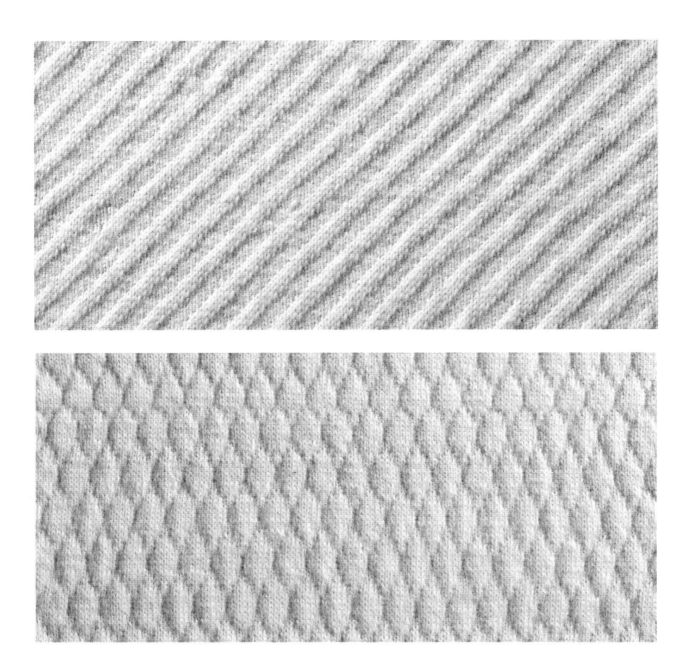

TOP: Change the stitches being slipped every row for a diagonal rib pattern: This is still a basic (k2, sl 2) fabric, but each RS row the pattern is shifted over by a stitch.

BOTTOM: Create more complex fabrics by working other patterns in slipped stitches. This fabric is based on Slipped Stitches and Stockinette #3 (see page 44), but the shape worked in slipped stitches is a vertically oriented oval.

TOP: Create a brocade-like fabric by changing the position of the slipped stitches every row. In this case, a 2-stitch rib of slipped stitches is moved over to the right and back to the left to create a wavy line.

BOTTOM: Work a few rows in plain stockinette between sections of a slipped stitch fabric to create checks.

SLIPPED STITCHES AND GARTER STITCH

Slipped stitches with garter stitch do not work as well for shadow patterns as with stockinette. The pattern looks as if it has two different garter stitches, one tight and the other loose. The tight one is really the purl side of the stockinette that stands out when the stitches are slipped on every other row.

This cardigan is created from the pattern Slipped Stitches and Garter Stitch #1 (see page 50). This sample has an unshaped body and drop sleeve with a simple crew neck following the garment template given on pages 208–209. The cuff and body edgings are worked on smaller needles. Stitches are picked up around the neckline, and a facing is worked so that when turned in and sewn down on the inside of the garment, the stockinette side shows.

Slipped Stitches and Garter Stitch #1

Stitch count: multiple of 6.

ROW 1 (WS): Knit.

ROW 2 (RS): *K2, sl 3 wyb, k1; rep from *.

Repeat Rows 1–2.

Slipped Stitches and Garter Stitch #2

Stitch count: multiple of 11.

ROWS 1–7: Knit.

ROWS 8, 10, 12, 14, 16, 18, AND 20 (RS): *K2, sl 7 wyb, k2; rep from *.

ROWS 9, 11, 13, 15, 17, AND 19 (WS): Knit.

ROWS 21 AND 22: Knit.

Repeat Rows 1–22.

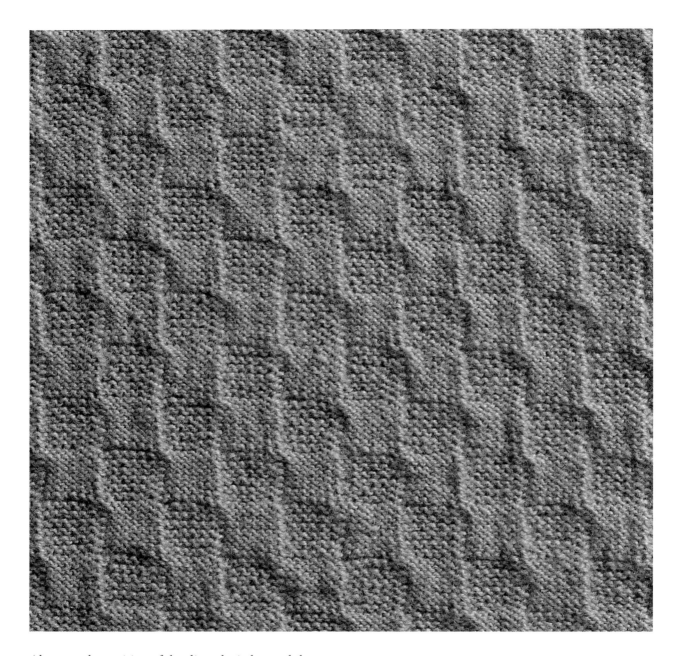

Alternate the position of the slipped stitches and the worked stitches to create blocks. In this swatch, the blocks are 6 stitches wide and twelve rows high.

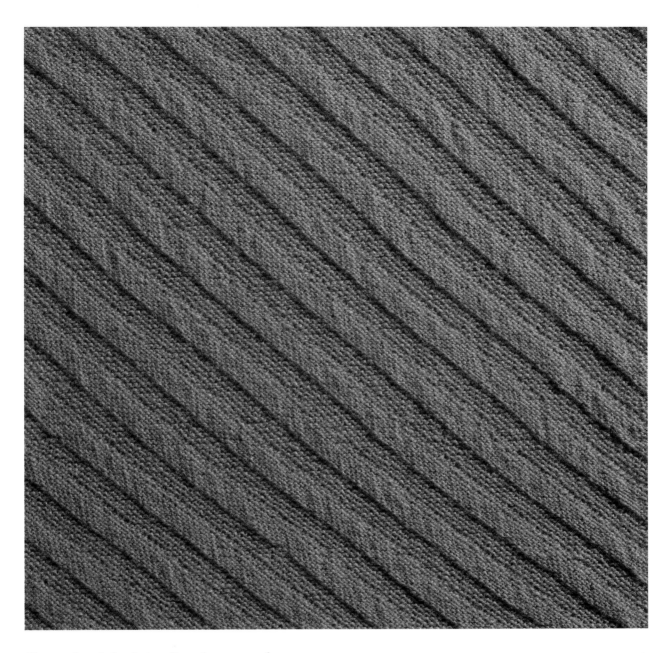

Change the stitches being slipped every row for a diagonal rib pattern: This is still a basic (k4, sl 4) fabric, but each RS row the pattern is shifted over by a stitch.

SLIPPED STITCHES TO FORM WELTS

When you slip every other stitch across a whole row for several rows and the yarn always strands in front of the slipped stitch on the right side, a welt develops. When you then work across all the stitches, they are forced together and the welt rises. The number of rows over which you can slip stitches is, of course, limited. If you want a larger welt, you can pick up stitches on the wrong side and work a few rows (fewer rows than for intended welt on RS). Then you hold both needles parallel and knit one stitch from the front needle together with one stitch from the back needle, across all the sts to join the sets.

This cardigan is created from the pattern Slipped Stitches to Form Welts #4 (see page 62). This sample has an unshaped body and drop sleeve with a simple crew neck following the garment template given on pages 208–209. Stitches are picked up around the neckline, and a facing is worked so that when turned in and sewn down on the inside of the garment, the stockinette side shows.

Slipped Stitches to Form Welts #1

Stitch count: multiple of 2 + 1.

ROW 1 (WS): *P1, sl 1 wyb; rep from * to last st p1.

ROW 2 (RS): K1, *sl 1 wyf, k1; rep from *.

ROW 3 (WS): Work as for Row 1.

ROW 4 (RS): Knit.

Repeat Rows 1–4.

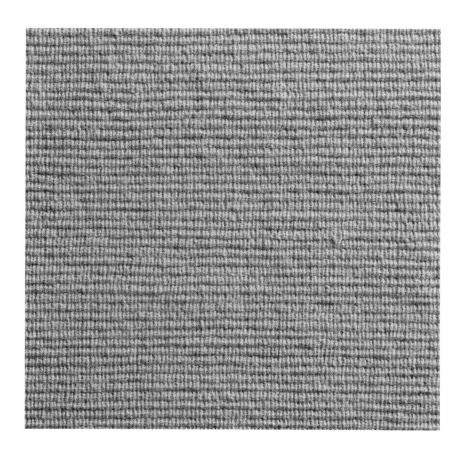

Slipped Stitches to Form Welts #2

Stitch count: multiple of 2 + 1.
Two colors.
CO with color 1.

ROWS 1, 3, AND 5 (WS): With color 1, *p1, sl 1 wyb; rep from * to last st p1.

ROWS 2 AND 4 (RS): With color 1, k1, *sl 1 wyf, k1; rep from *.

ROW 6 (RS): With color 1, knit.

ROWS 7, 9, AND 11 (WS): With color 2, *p1, sl 1 wyb; rep from * to last st p1.

ROWS 8 AND 10 (RS): With color 2, k1, *sl 1 wyf, k1; rep from *.

ROW 12 (RS): With color 2, knit.

Repeat Rows 1–12.

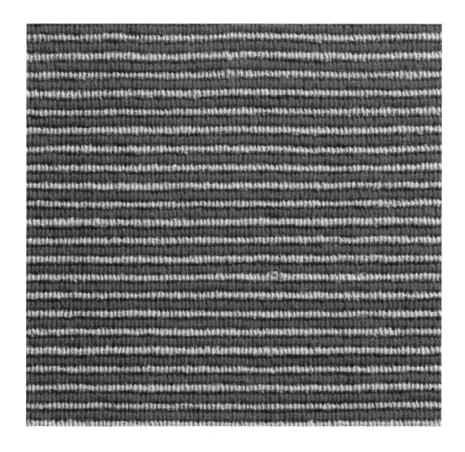

Work more plain stockinette stitch rows between the welts to change the look.

TOP ROW: Work in one color and work three or more rows of stockinette between the welts.

BOTTOM LEFT: Work in two colors and work three rows of stockinette between the welts.

BOTTOM RIGHT: Work in one color and work a section of plain stockinette between groups of welts.

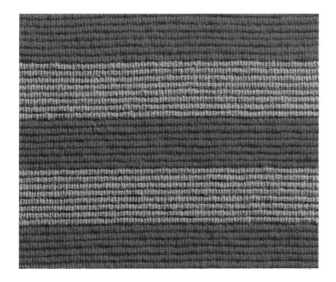

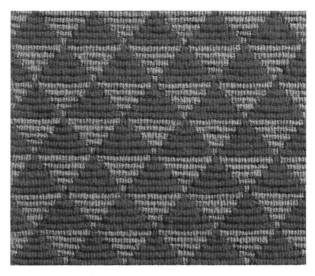

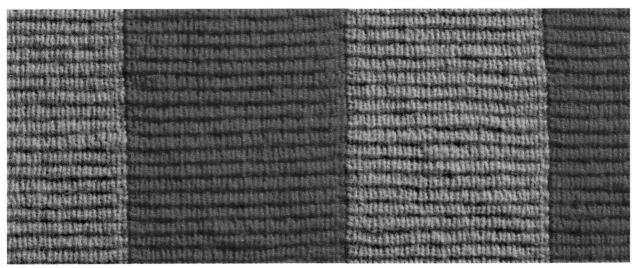

TOP LEFT: Work as for Slipped Stitches to Form Welts #2 (see page 57), but work eight welts in one color before changing to the other.

TOP RIGHT: Work as for Slipped Stitches to Form Welts #3 (see page 60), but create triangle shapes in alternating colors. Work a 10-stitch repeat across the rows, starting with one st in color 1 and nine in color 2, and work 2 more stitches in color 1 every RS row until you have 9 in color 1 and 1 in color 2. Shift the position of the triangles over by 10 stitches to create a tessellated look.

BOTTOM: Work as for Slipped Stitches to Form Welts #1 (see page 56), creating vertical stripes by alternating two colors across the row with the intarsia method (see page 207).

Slipped Stitches to Form Welts #3

Stitch count: multiple of 48.

Two colors.

For information about intarsia, see the Techniques section (page 207).

CO with color 1.

ROW 1 (WS): *With color 1, p1, sl 1 wyb; rep from *.

ROW 2 (RS): *With color 1, sl 1 wyf, k1; rep from *.

ROW 3 (WS): Work as for Row 1.

ROW 4 (RS): With color 1, knit.

ROW 5 (WS): *With color 1, (p1, sl 1 wyb) 4 times. With color 2, (p1, sl 1 wyb) 5 times. With color 1, (p1, sl 1 wyb) 15 times; rep from *.

ROW 6 (RS): *With color 1, (sl 1 wyf, k1) 15 times. With color 2, (sl 1 wyf, k1) 5 times. With color 1, (sl 1 wyf, k1) 4 times; rep from *.

ROW 7 (WS): Work as for Row 5.

ROW 8 (RS): *With color 1, k30. With color 2, k10. With color 1, k8; rep from *.

ROW 9 (WS): *With color 1, (p1, sl 1 wyb) 3 times. With color 2, (p1, sl 1 wyb) 7 times. With color 1, (p1, sl 1 wyb) 14 times; rep from *.

ROW 10 (RS): *With color 1, (sl 1 wyf, k1) 14 times. With color 2, (sl 1 wyf, k1) 7 times. With color 1, (sl 1 wyf, k1) 3 times; rep from *.

ROW 11 (WS): Work as for Row 9.

ROW 12 (RS): *With color 1, k28. With color 2, k14. With color 1, k6; rep from *.

ROW 13 (WS): *With color 1, (p1, sl 1 wyb) 2 times. With color 2, (p1, sl 1 wyb) 9 times. With color 1, (p1, sl 1 wyb) 13 times; rep from *.

ROW 14 (RS): *With color 1, (sl 1 wyf, k1) 13 times. With color 2, (sl 1 wyf, k1) 9 times. With color 1, (sl 1 wyf, k1) 2 times; rep from *.

ROW 15 (WS): Work as for Row 13.

ROW 16 (RS): *With color 1, k26. With color 2, k18. With color 1, k4; rep from *.

Work Rows 13–16 twice more.

Work Rows 9–12.

Work Row 5–8.

Work Rows 1–4.

ROW 37 (RS): *With color 1, (p1, sl 1 wyb) 16 times. With color 2, (p1, sl 1 wyb) 5 times. With color 1, (p1, sl 1 wyb) 3 times; rep from *.

ROW 38 (WS): *With color 1, (sl 1 wyf, k1) 3 times. With color 2, (sl 1 wyf, k1) 5 times. With color 1, (sl 1 wyf, k1) 16 times; rep from *.

ROW 39 (RS): Work as for Row 37.

ROW 40 (WS): *With color 1, k6. With color 2, k10. With color 1, k32; rep from *.

ROW 41 (RS): *With color 1, (p1, sl 1 wyb) 15 times. With color 2, (p1, sl 1 wyb) 7 times. With color 1, (p1, sl 1 wyb) 2 times; rep from *.

ROW 42 (WS): *With color 1, (sl 1 wyf, k1) 2 times. With color 2, (sl 1 wyf, k1) 7 times. With color 1, (sl 1 wyf, k1) 15 times; rep from *.

ROW 43 (RS): Work as for Row 41.

ROW 44 (WS): *With color 1, k4. With color 2, k14. With color 1, k30; rep from *.

ROW 45 (RS): *With color 1, (p1, sl 1 wyb) 14 times. With color 2, (p1, sl 1 wyb) 9 times. With color 1, p1, sl 1 wyb; rep from *.

ROW 46 (WS): *With color 1, sl 1 wyf, k1). With color 2, (sl 1 wyf, k1) 9 times. With color 1, (sl 1 wyf, k1) 14 times; rep from *.

ROW 47 (RS): Work as for Row 45.

ROW 48 (WS): *With color 1, k2. With color 2, k18. With color 1, k28; rep from *.

Work Rows 45–48 twice more.

Work Rows 41–44.

Work Rows 37–40.

Repeat Rows 1–64.

Slipped Stitches to Form Welts #4

Stitch count: multiple of 2 + 1.
Three colors.
CO with color 1.

ROW 1 (WS): With color 1, knit.

ROW 2 (RS): With color 2, knit.

ROWS 3, 5, AND 7 (WS): With color 2, *p1, sl 1 wyb, p1; rep from *.

ROWS 4 AND 6 (RS): With color 2, k1, *sl 1 wyf, k1; rep from *.

ROWS 8 AND 9: With color 1, knit.

ROW 10 (RS): With color 3, knit, wrapping the yarn twice around the needle before bringing through to knit stitch.

ROW 11 (WS): With color 3, purl, letting extra loop drop off needle.

ROW 12 (RS): With color 1, knit.

Repeat Rows 1–12.

The same technique can create wildly different fabrics.

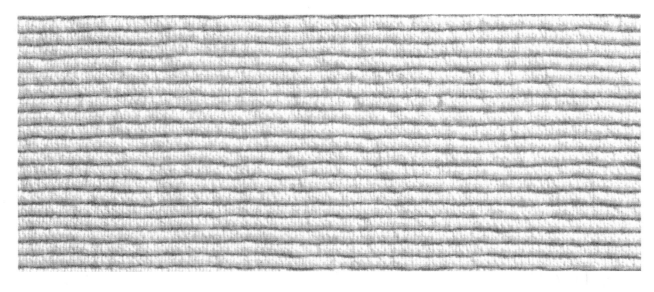

TOP: Slipped Stitches to Form Welts #1 (see page 56) worked in a single color. Deeper welts are created by working an extra pair of rows of the slipping pattern.

BOTTOM: Create multicolored patterns on deeper welts using the instarsia technique. Join the first two contrasting colors on the WS and purl across, alternating colors as you wish. Then work two rows of the welt pattern in the two colors as set. Add in a third contrasting color and create vertical stripes by slipping stitches in the first two contrasting colors and working the third contrasting color in stockinette stitch. Wide stripes of plain stockinette between the welts provide great emphasis.

OPPOSITE PAGE: Welts can be used to divide up other elements of a patterned fabric. In this example, contrasting color welts are used to divide up fabric with relief blocks and stripes worked in reverse stockinette stitch with intarsia sections.

SLIPPED STITCHES TO FORM WELTS ON THE WRONG SIDE

Sometimes, when I'm knitting, I discover that an attractive pattern is developing on the wrong side of the fabric. Wrong side welts are an uncommon, discrete surface pattern. Right and wrong sides can also be combined to shape blocks and stripes.

Slipped Stitches to Form Welts on the Wrong Side #1

Stitch count: multiple of 2 + 1.
Two colors.
CO with color 1.

ROW 1 (WS): With color 1, knit.

ROW 2 (RS): With color 1, purl.

ROW 3 (WS): With color 2, *k1, sl 1 wyf; rep from * to last st, k1.

ROW 4 (RS): With color 2, p1, *sl 1 wyb, p1; rep from *.

ROW 5 (WS): With color 2, work as for Row 3.

ROW 6 (RS): With color 2, work as for Row 4.

Repeat Rows 1–6.

Work the pattern Slipped Stitches to Form Welts on
the Wrong Side #1 (see page 68) with only one color for
a very different but equally interesting fabric.

Repeat Rows 1–18 only of the pattern Slipped Stitches
to Form Welts on the Wrong Side #2 (see page 72).

Slipped Stitches to Form Welts on the Wrong Side #2

Stitch count: multiple of 14.
Two colors.
CO with color 1.

ROW 1 (WS): With color 1, *(p1, sl 1 wyb) 3 times, p1, (k1, sl 1 wyf) 3 times, k1; rep from *.

ROW 2 (RS): With color 1, *(p1, sl 1 wyb) 3 times, p1, (k1, sl 1 wyf) 3 times, k1; rep from *.

ROW 3 (WS): With color 1, work as for Row 1.

ROW 4 (RS): With color 1, work as for Row 2.

ROW 5 (WS): With color 2, *p7, k7; rep from *.

ROW 6 (RS): With color 2, *p7, k7; rep from *.

Work Rows 1–6 twice more.

ROW 19 (WS): With color 1, *(k1, sl 1 wyf) 3 times, k1, (p1, sl 1 wyb) 3 times, p1; rep from *.

ROW 20 (RS): With color 1, *(k1, sl 1 wyf) 3 times, k1, (p1, sl 1 wyb) 3 times, p1; rep from *.

ROW 21 (WS): With color 1, work as for Row 7.

ROW 22 (RS): With color 1, work as for Row 8.

ROW 23 (WS): With color 2, *k7, p7; rep from *.

ROW 24 (RS): With color 2, *k7, p7; rep from *.

Work Rows 19–24 twice more.

Repeat Rows 1–36.

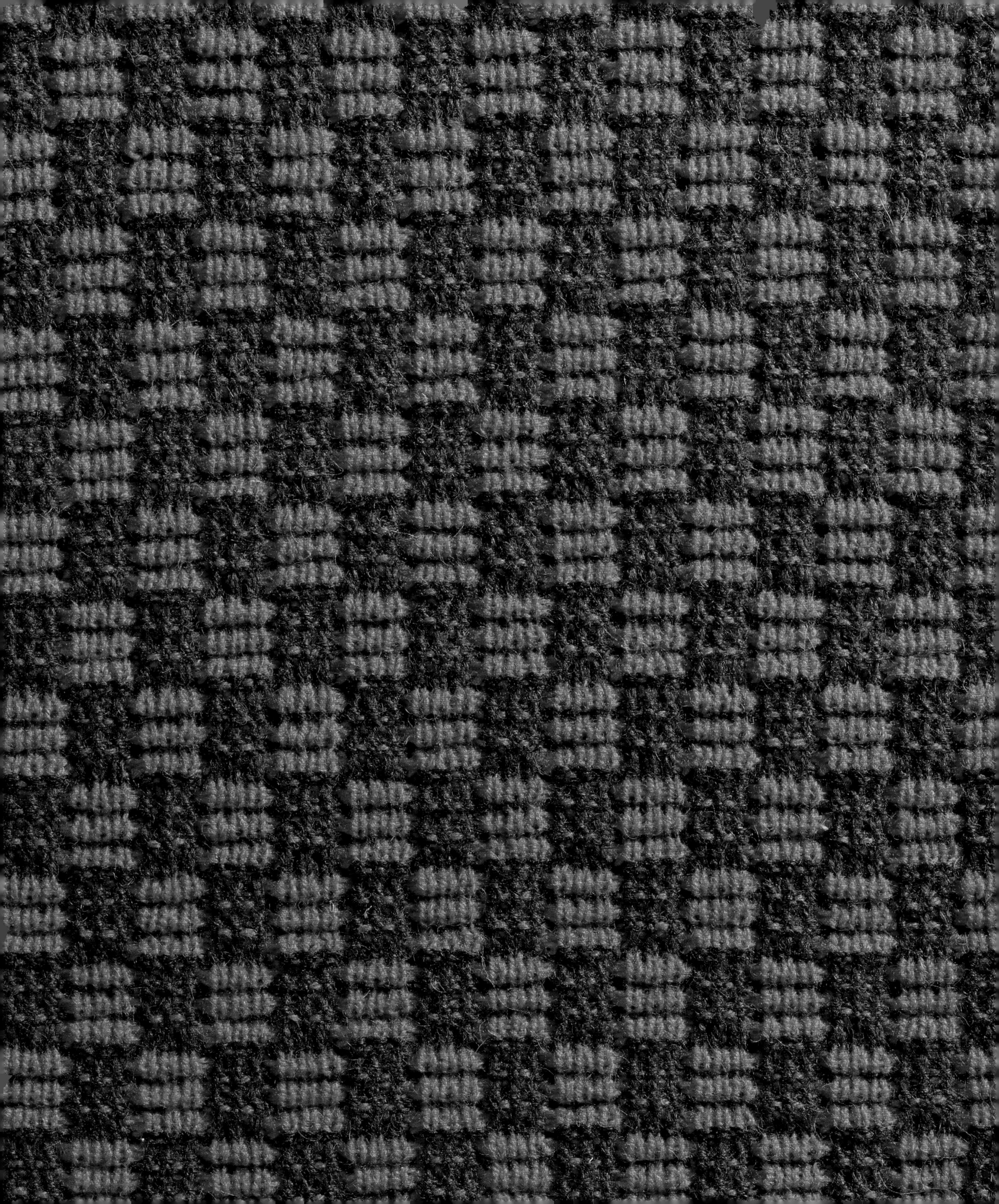

CASTING ON AND BINDING OFF WITHIN A ROW 1

If you cast on stitches partway through a row, and, almost always, immediately bind them off, you can make little hooks or long cords. Everything depends on how many stitches you cast on. These hooks and cords can be arranged in various ways by, for example, binding them with a knot, joining pairs, or joining several hooks or cords.

Casting On and Binding Off within a Row 1: #1

Stitch count: multiple of 16.

ROWS 1–11: Work in stockinette, beginning on WS with a purl row.

ROW 12 (RS): *K7, CO 8 sts (K-CO = *knit 1 st, leaving old st on left needle, twist the new stitch and place on left needle; rep from *), BO the new 8 sts, k8; rep from *.

ROWS 13–23: Work in stockinette, beginning on WS with a purl row.

ROW 24 (RS): *K15, K-CO 8 sts, BO the 8 new sts; rep from *.

Repeat Rows 1–24.

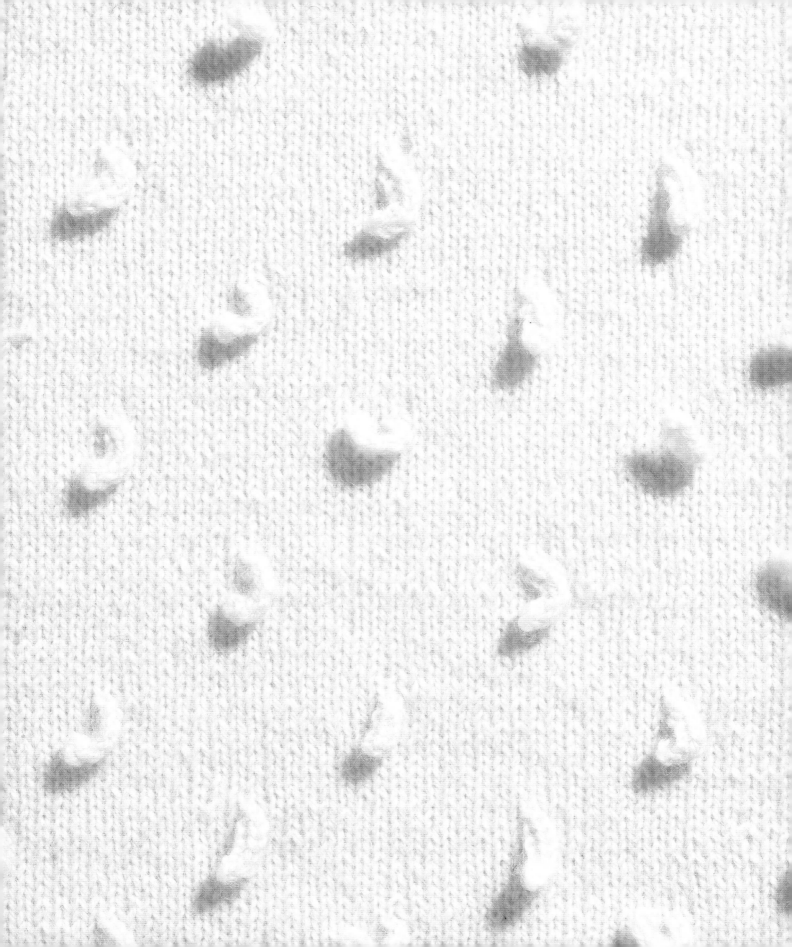

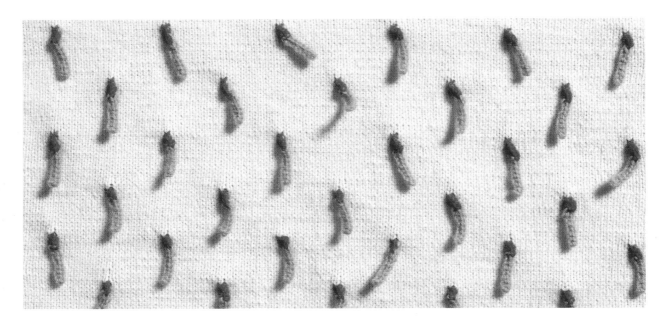

TOP: Work the first few stitches of the cord in one contrasting color and the rest in a second.

BOTTOM: Work a few rows of garter stitch on the cast-on stitches, alternating colors, casting off a stitch or two at the start of every wrong-side row.

OPPOSITE PAGE: Work three cords on adjacent stitches, using different colors. Use a fourth color to work the base stitch of the center cord.

This pattern lends itself to easy variations.

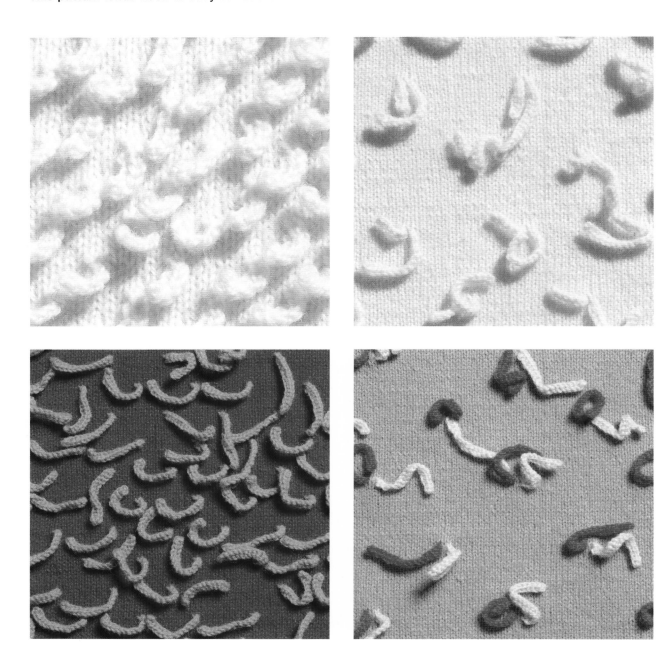

TOP LEFT: The cords are worked close together, every four rows.

TOP RIGHT: Work two cords on adjacent stitches.

BOTTOM LEFT: Work the cords in a contrasting color, randomly placed on the fabric.

BOTTOM RIGHT: Work two longer cords, one stitch apart, in different contrasting colors.

Work cords very close together in multiple colors for different effects.

Casting On and Binding Off within a Row 1: #2

Stitch count: multiple of 70.

ROWS 1–3: Work in stockinette, beginning on WS with a purl row.

Now work following the chart.

Squares filled with an X or dot: K-CO 8 (K-CO = *knit 1 st, leaving old st on left needle, twist the new stitch and place on left needle; rep from *), and immediately BO the new 8 sts.

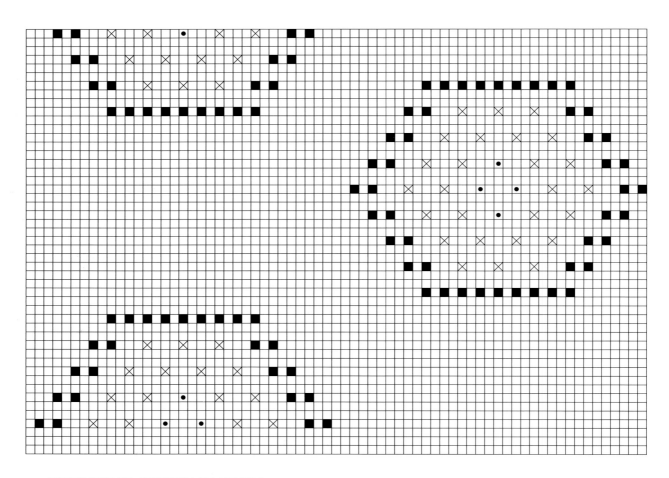

EMPTY SQUARE= STOCKINETTE, COLOR 1.

FILLED SQUARE= CO/BO WITH COLOR 2.

SQUARE WITH X= CO/BO WITH COLOR 3.

SQUARE WITH DOT= CO/BO WITH COLOR 4.

Knotting together two cords changes the look significantly. Work the two cords close together in the same color as the background, or space them apart further and work them in different colors.

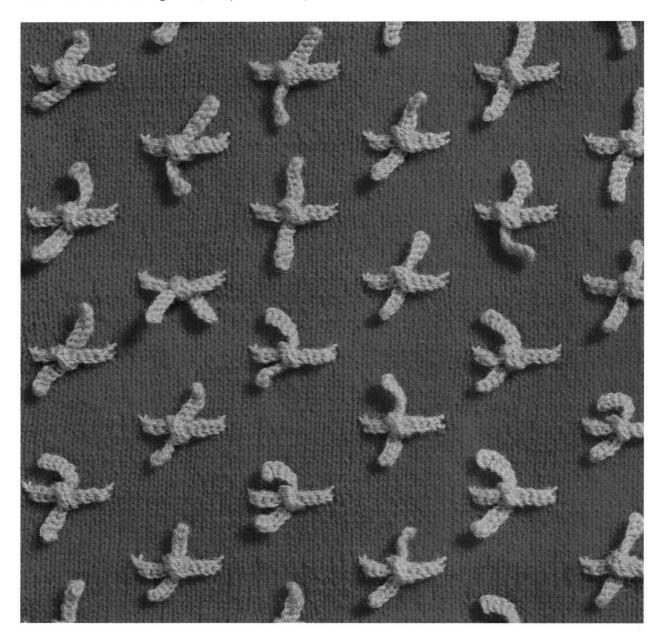

THIS PAGE: Create more regular and linear knots by working the cords on the same row, a few stitches apart, in a single contrasting color.

OPPOSITE PAGE, TOP: Work two longer cords a few rows and stitches apart. Tie them together.

OPPOSITE PAGE, BOTTOM: As above, but work the cords in different contrasting color.

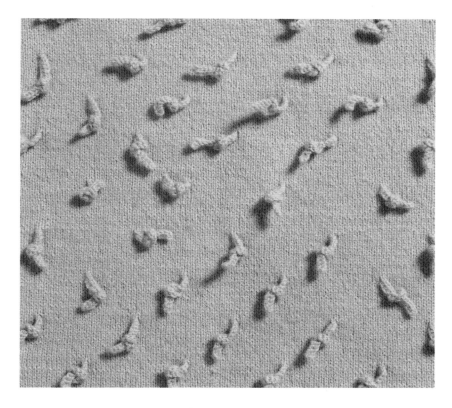

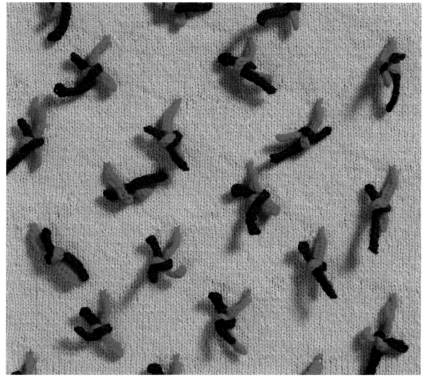

Casting On and Binding Off within a Row 1: #3

Stitch count: multiple of 44.
Three colors.
You'll need an extra needle.
CO with color 1.

ROWS 1–25: Garter st.

ROW 26 (RS): *With color 1, k4.

With color 2, K-CO 20 sts (K-CO = *knit 1 st, leaving old st on left needle, twist the new stitch and place on left needle; rep from *), using extra needle. BO 20. Slip st from extra needle to right needle.

With color 1, k12.

With color 3, K-CO 20, using extra needle. BO 20.

Slip the st from extra needle to right needle.

With color 1, k26; rep from *.

Tie the two little cords together with a square knot.

ROW 27 (WS): Knit across except for the sts in contrast color (colors 2 and 3), which should be purled.

ROWS 28–51: Garter stitch.

ROW 52 (RS): *With color 1, k26.

With color 2, K-CO 20 sts, rep from *, using extra needle. BO 20. Slip sts from extra needle to right needle.

With color 1, k12.

With color 3, K-CO 20, using extra needle. BO 20.

Slip the sts from extra needle to right needle.

With color 1, k4; rep from *.

Tie the two little cords together with a square knot.

ROW 53 (WS): Work as for Row 27.

Repeat Rows 2–53.

CASTING ON AND BINDING OFF WITHIN A ROW 2

When you use this technique to make hooks and cords that pop right out from the knitting, you can vary the effect by knitting them together with the background fabric in a different spot from where they originally popped up. Several hooks and cords can be stacked and braided with each other so that a new shape develops.

Casting On and Binding Off within a Row 2: #1

Stitch count: multiple of 20.

ROWS 1–19: Work in stockinette, beginning on WS with a purl row.

ROW 20 (RS): *With color 1, k8.

With color 2, K-CO 6 (K-CO = *knit 1 st, leaving old st on left needle, twist the new stitch and place on left needle; rep from *), BO 6.

With color 1, k2.

With color 2, K-CO 6; rep from *, BO 6.

With color 1, k8; rep from *.

ROWS 21–25: Work in stockinette, beginning on WS with a purl row.

ROW 26 (RS): *K8, (place the outermost st of cord onto left needle and knit it together through back loop with the next st), k2, (place the outermost st of cord onto left needle and knit it together through back loop with the next st), k8; rep from *.

Repeat Rows 1–26.

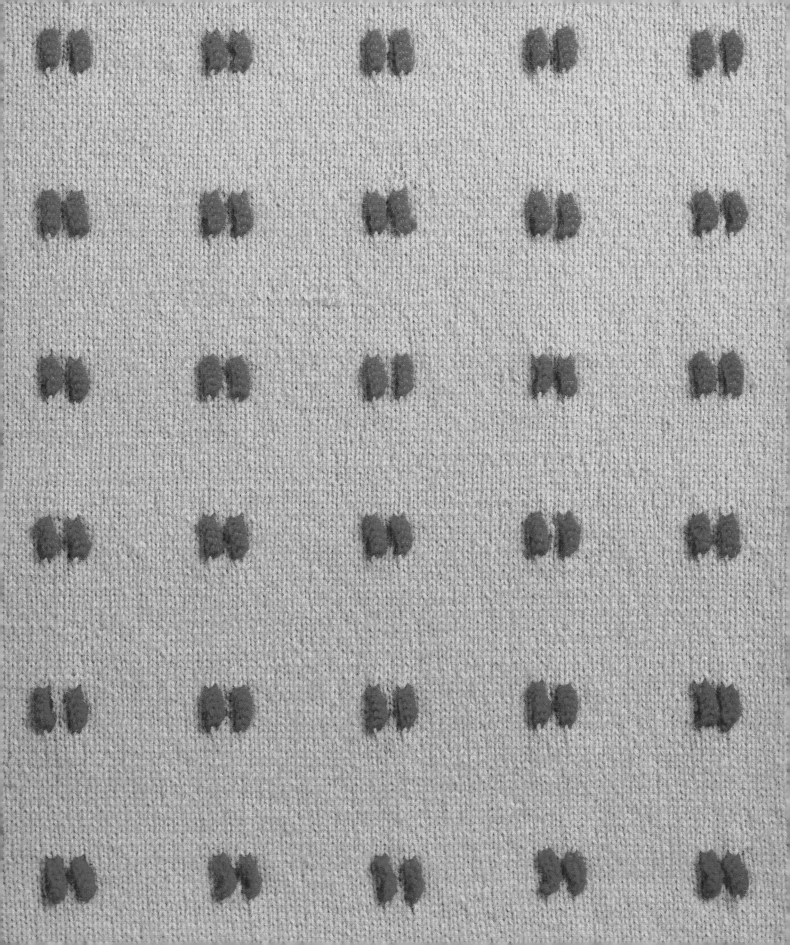

Casting On and Binding Off within a Row 2: #2

Stitch count: multiple of 18.
You'll need an extra needle.

ROWS 1–9: With color 1, work in stockinette, beginning on WS with a purl row.

ROW 10 (RS): *With color 1, k5.

With color 2, K-CO 8 sts (K-CO = *knit 1 st, leaving old st on left needle, twist the new stitch and place on left needle; rep from *), using extra needle. BO 8. Slip sts from extra needle to right needle.

With color 1, k12; rep from *.

ROWS 11–13: With color 1, work in stockinette, beginning on WS with a purl row.

ROW 14 (RS): *With color 1, k3.

With color 2, K-CO 6 sts, BO 6.

With color 1, k3.

With color 2, K-CO 6 sts, BO 6.

With color 1, k10; rep from *.

ROWS 15–19: With color 1, work in stockinette, beginning on WS with a purl row.

ROW 20 (RS): With color 1, *K4, (place outermost st of next cord onto left needle and knit together through back loop with the next st) 3 times, k11; rep from *.

ROW 21 (WS): With color 1, purl.

ROW 22 (RS): *With color 1, k2.

With color 3, K-CO 14 sts, using extra needle, BO 14, knitting the last st before the final bind off with color 1.

Slip sts from extra needle to right needle.

With color 1, k5, bring the cord in color 3 under the three cords in color 1 and place the outermost st on left needle and knit together through back loop with next st, k9; rep from *.

ROWS 23–31: With color 1, work in stockinette, beginning on WS with a purl row.

ROW 32 (RS): *With color 1, k14.

With color 2, K-CO 8 sts using extra needle. BO 8. Slip sts from extra needle to right needle.

With color 1, k3; rep from *.

ROWS 33–35: With color 1, work in stockinette, beginning on WS with a purl row.

ROW 36 (RS): *With color 1, k12.

With color 2, K-CO 6 sts, BO 6.

With color 1, k3.

With color 2, K-CO 6 sts, BO 6.

With color 1, k1; rep from *.

ROWS 37–41: With color 1, work in stockinette, beginning on WS with a purl row.

ROW 42 (RS): With color 1, *K13, (place outermost st of next cord onto left needle and knit together through back loop with the next st) 3 times, k2; rep from *.

ROW 43 (WS): With color 1, purl.

ROW 44 (RS): *With color 1, k11.

With color 3, K-CO 14 with extra needle.

BO 14, knitting the last st before final bind off with color 1.

Slip sts from extra needle to right needle.

With color 1, k5, bring the cord in color 3 under the three cords in color 1 and place the outermost st on left needle and knit together through back loop with next st; rep from *.

Repeat Rows 1–44.

CORDS ALONG OUTER EDGE OF KNITTING

This technique is a decorative way to join smaller knitted pieces or a complete garment and can be worked so that a pattern forms. Although it can be worked as casting on and casting off, in the case of these examples, it is worked with a crochet hook. The end result is the same.

This cardigan is constructed from simple garter stitch pieces worked with an unshaped body and drop sleeve with a simple crew neck following the garment template given on pages 208–209. Only the shoulder seams are sewn together in the traditional manner; to join the sleeves to the body and to join the sides and close the sleeves, cords are worked at regular intervals along the edges and tied together. Two contrasting color-striped garter stitch cords are worked at the sides of the neck opening.

Cords Along Outer Edge of Knitting #1

The technique is double-knit stockinette.
Seed and garter stitch are also suitable techniques.
Here's a sample knit with three bands.

CO 16 sts. You need an even number of stitches for double knitting.

ALL ROWS: *K1, sl 1 wyf; rep from *.

Make 3 bands as set, each 4¼" (11 cm) long.

BINDING OFF (WORK LOOSELY): K1, *k2tog, psso; rep from * to last st, k1. Cut yarn and pull through final st to secure.

Crochet a cord attached to side of band beginning ¾" (2 cm) from lower edge as follows:

Ch 18, turn and sc 18 across chain.

Crochet a second cord about 3½" (9 cm) from lower edge.

Repeat as shown on drawing.

Tie bands together with square knots.

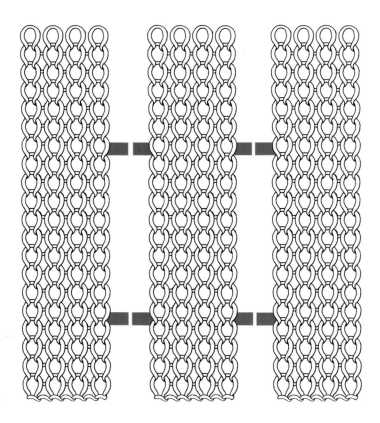

Cords Along Outer Edge of Knitting #2

The technique is double-knit stockinette.
Seed and garter stitch are also suitable techniques.
Here's a sample knit with four blocks.

CO 40 sts. You need an even number of stitches for double knitting.

ALL ROWS: *K1, sl 1 wyf; rep from *.

Make four square blocks.

BINDING OFF (WORK LOOSELY): K1, *k2tog, psso; rep from * to last st, k1. Cut yarn and pull through final st to secure.

Crochet a cord at each corner of each block as follows:

Ch 18, turn and sc 18 across chain.

Use the yarn tails to sew the four cords at each intersection together.

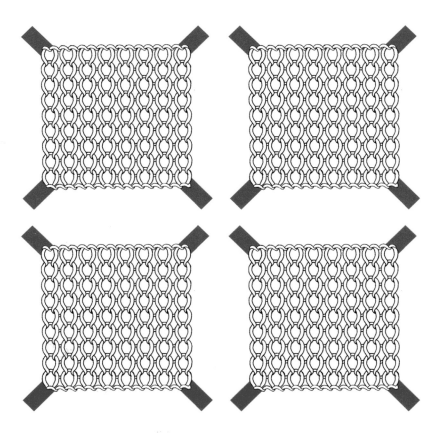

THE CHART SHOWS THE PATTERN ON THE RIGHT SIDE.

THIS PAGE: Work cords in contrasting colors at the edges of other shapes, e.g., small crosses as worked in Knitting in Different Directions #2 (see page 184). Knot them together to create a fascinating openwork fabric.

OPPOSITE PAGE: Create a larger pattern by working cords both on and at the sides of a piece, in multiple colors. Once the strips of knitting have been worked, lay them out to plan the positions of the cords and the knots.

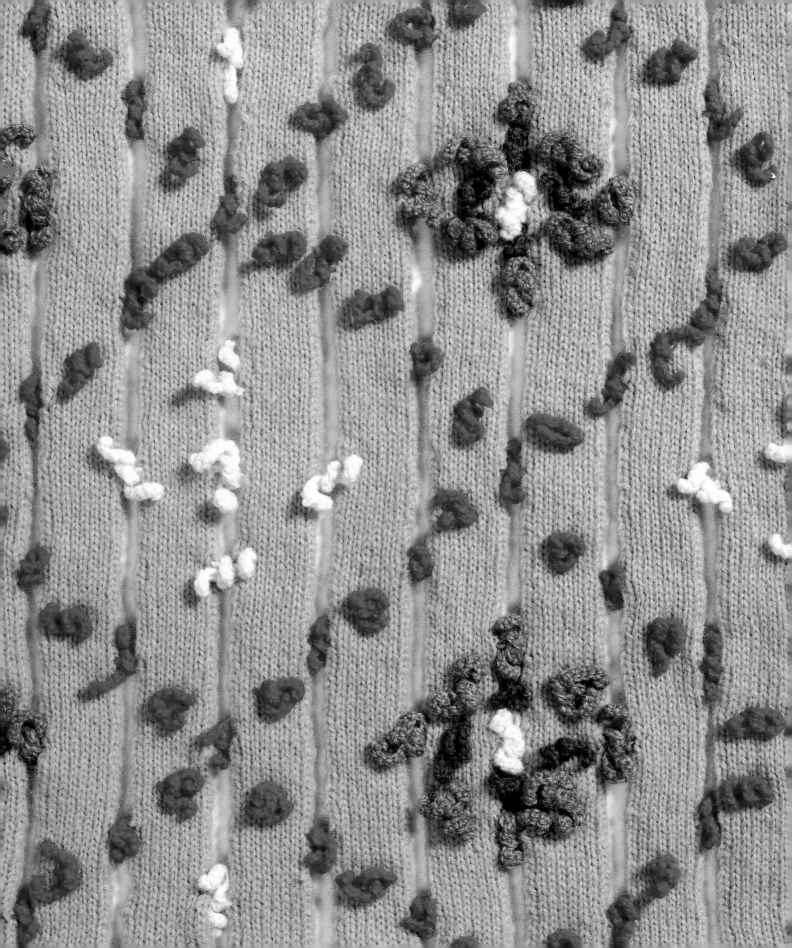

A basic drop sleeve sweater is created from long narrow strips of garter stitch, lying lengthwise, tied together with cords worked in a contrasting color. Draw a schematic and plan the pieces of the garment as per the template given on pages 208–209. Work long narrow garter stitch strips to conform to the dimensions. The lower body strips are worked for the full circumference of the body, and the cast-on and bound-off edges seamed together. The opening for the neck is square, created by simply working two shorter strips for the sleeves at the top of the front.

PATTERNS ON
BIND-OFF ROWS

As every knitter knows, a nice little chain is made when you bind off. I've made a striped pattern with this bind-off chain. Of course, you can make several other pattern arrangements by stopping the bind off and working the background knitting between the desired pattern shapes. In order to continue knitting after the stitches have disappeared with the bind off, pick up new stitches from the wrong side. The stitches I put on the needle are those that lie closest to the bind-off chain.

Bind-Off Row Pattern #1

Variation 1—one color.

ROWS 1–7: Work in stockinette, beginning on WS with a purl row.

ROW 8 (RS): BO all the stitches; 1 st rems. Turn.

Pick up and purl 1 st; lift st rem from previous row over the picked-up st to bind it off; continue, picking up and purling until you have the same number of stitches as bound off. *Note:* Pick up the stitches closest to the bind-off chain.

Repeat Rows 1–8.

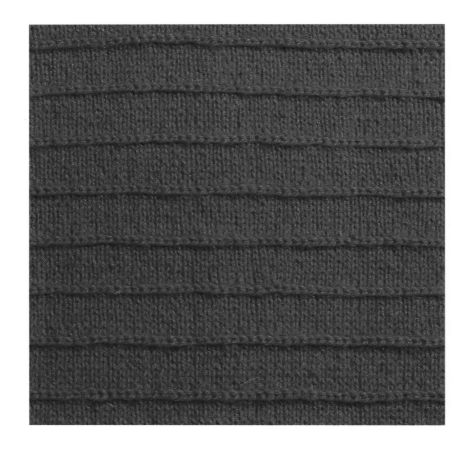

Bind-Off Row Pattern #2

Variation 2—two colors.

ROWS 1–7: Work in stockinette, beginning on WS with a purl row.

ROW 8 (RS): With color 2, BO all the stitches; 1 st rems. Turn.

With color 1, pick up and purl 1 st (using the strand in color 1); lift st rem from previous row over the picked-up st to bind it off; continue, picking up and purling the strands in color 1 until you have the same number of stitches as bound off.

ROW 9 (RS): With color 1, knit.

Repeat Rows 1–9.

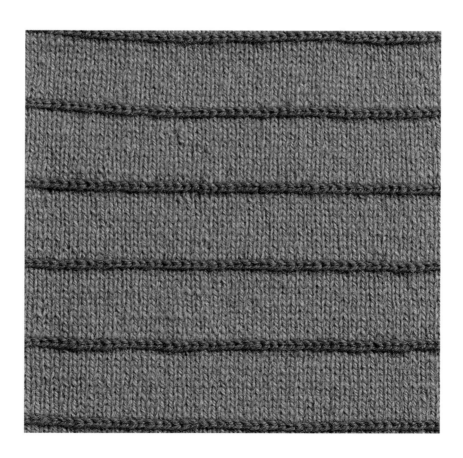

Bind-Off Row Pattern #3

Variation 3—three colors.

ROWS 1–7: With color 1, work in stockinette, beginning on WS with a purl row.

ROW 8 (RS): With colors 2 and 3, BO all the stitches, alternating sts with colors 2 and 3; 1 st rems. Turn.

With color 1, pick up and purl 1 st (using the strand in color 1); lift st rem from previous row over the picked-up st to bind it off; continue, picking up and purling the strands in color 1 until you have the same number of stitches as bound off.

ROW 9 (RS): With color 1, knit.

Repeat Rows 1–9.

Bind-Off Row Pattern #4

Variation 4—striped background and unlimited number of colors.

The pattern consists of two-color braids against horizontal stripes of the background color. The colors can be changed at the beginning of every pattern repeat (on Row 2) if desired.

ROWS 1–7: With color 1, work in stockinette, beginning on WS with a purl row.

ROW 8 (RS): With colors 2 and 3, BO all the stitches, alternating sts with colors 2 and 3; 1 st rem. Turn.

With color 1, pick up and purl 1 st (using the strand in color 1); lift st rem from previous row over the picked-up st to bind it off; continue, picking up and purling the strands in color 1 until you have the same number of stitches as bound off.

ROWS 9–14: With color 1, work in stockinette, beginning on RS with a knit row.

Change colors and repeat Rows 2–14.

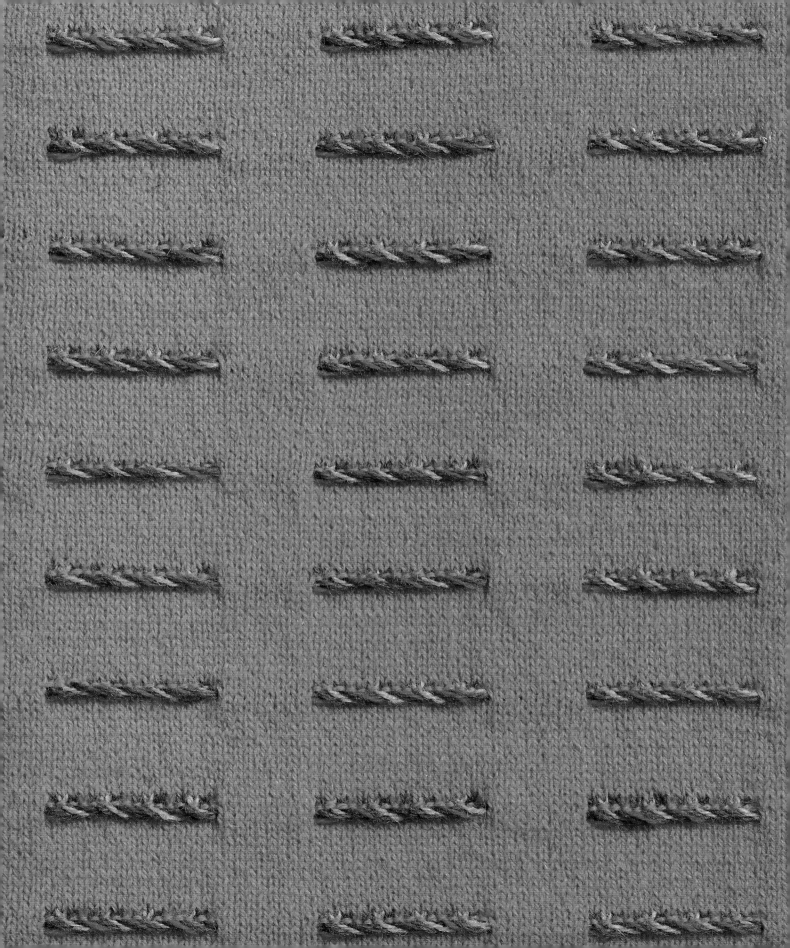

BRAIDS

My braid rows have been "stolen" from two-end (or twined) knitting. What I call braid rows are purl stitches and rows in two-end knitting. They are worked with two strands of yarn (one end from the outside of a yarn ball and the other strand from the inside of the ball) on the right side of the fabric, either in the same color or two different colors. The yarn ends twist around each other on every stitch. I have tried the technique in "regular" knitting with several colors, sometimes even three, four, five, and six colors. However, when there are several colors, the floats on the wrong side are too long.

In other types of pattern design that are not striped, the yarns float on the wrong side when they are not being knit into the pattern. Technically, those designs are similar to two-color stranded knitting. Before and between the braid rows you can work as many stockinette rows as you like. The braid is formed on the right side of the knitting with all the yarn colors remaining on the right side.

Braid Row #1

Stitch count: multiple of 6.
Six colors.

Before and between the cord rows, work as many stockinette rows as you like. The cord is formed on the right side of the knitting with all the yarn colors remaining on the right side.

BRAID ROW (RS): *P1 with color 1, p1 with color 2, p1 with color 3, p1 with color 4, p1 with color 5, p1 with color 6; rep from *.

Braid Row #2

Stitch count: multiple of 3.
Three colors.

Before and between the cord rows, work as many stockinette rows as you like. The cord is formed on the right side of the knitting with all the yarn colors remaining on the right side.

BRAID ROW (RS): *P1 with color 1, p1 with color 2, p1 with color 3; rep from *.

Braid Row #3

Stitch count: multiple of 25.
Four colors.

The yarn is cut after every cord row unless you are knitting in the round.

The instructions are for working back and forth.

ROWS 1–7: Work in stockinette, beginning in WS with a purl row.

ROW 8 (RS): * K5, (p1 with color 1, p1 with color 2, p1 with color 3, p1 with color 4) 4 times, k4; rep from *.

ROWS 9–14: Work in stockinette, beginning on WS with a purl row.

Repeat Rows 1–14.

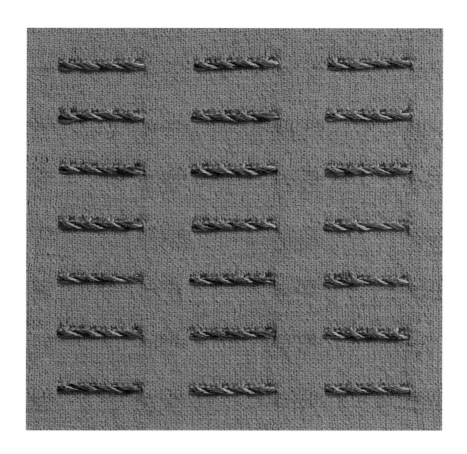

HONEYCOMB

Honeycomb is the name of a weaving technique many have tried after it was translated for knitting. The idea for the pattern shown here was conceived from the block stripes that I made honeycomb-fashion by joining the bands with slipped stitches. The next idea was, instead of slipping stitches, to go down six to eight rows in the knitting, pick up a stitch and knit it together with the nearest stitch on the current row.

This cardigan is worked with an unshaped body and drop sleeve with a simple crewneck following the garment template given on pages 208–209. The fabric is worked as per Honeycomb #1 (see page 120), with the WS facing. Stitches are picked up around the neckline, and a facing is worked so that when turned in and sewn down on the inside of the garment, the stockinette side shows.

Honeycomb #1

Stitch count: multiple of 10.
Two colors.

ROW 1 (WS): With color 1, purl.

ROW 2 (RS): With color 2, knit.

ROW 3 (WS): With color 2, knit.

ROWS 4–9: With color 1, work in stockinette, beginning with a knit row.

ROW 10 (RS): With color 2, *(pick up 1 st in color 2 from Row 2 and place it on left needle. Knit that stitch together with next st through back loop) 3 times, k7; rep from *.

ROW 11 (WS): With color 2, knit.

ROWS 12–17: With color 1, work in stockinette, beginning with a knit row.

ROW 18 (RS): With color 2, *k5, (pick up 1 st as in Row 9) 3 times, k2; rep from *.

ROW 19 (WS): With color 2, knit.

Repeat Rows 4–19.

OPPOSITE PAGE, TOP: WS

OPPOSITE PAGE, BOTTOM: RS

Honeycomb #2

Stitch count: multiple of 22.
Two colors.

ROWS 1–15: With color 1, work in stockinette, beginning on WS with a purl row.

ROW 16 (RS): With color 2, *(pick up 1 st 7 rows below and place it on left needle. Purl that stitch together with next st) 3 times, p16, (pick up 1 st 7 rows below and place it on left needle. Purl that stitch together with next st) 3 times; rep from *.

ROW 17 (WS): With color 2, knit.

ROW 18 (RS): With color 1, purl.

ROWS 19–25: With color 1, work in stockinette, beginning on WS with a purl row.

ROW 26 (RS): With color 1, *k8, (pick up 1 st 7 rows down and place it on left needle. Knit it together with next st) 6 times, k8; rep from *.

ROWS 27–32: With color 1, work in stockinette, beginning on WS with a purl row.

Repeat Rows 1–32.

The wrong sides of these fabrics are just as interesting.

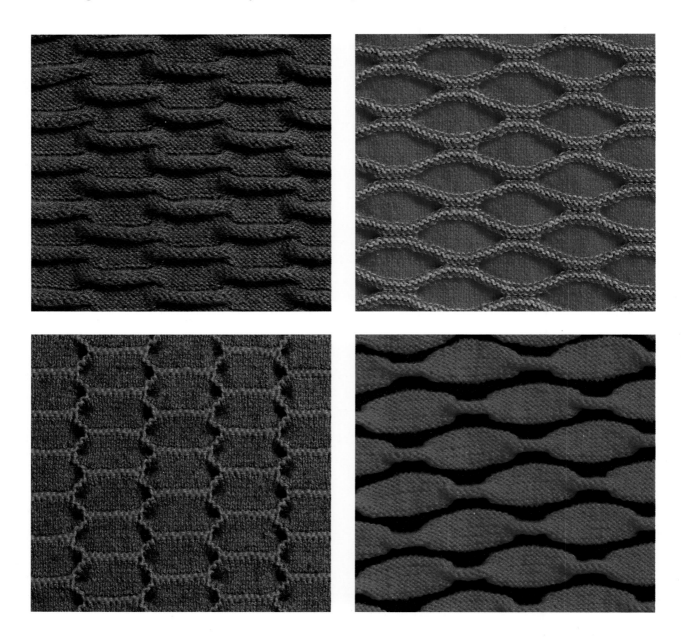

TOP LEFT: The wrong side of the bottom left swatch.

TOP RIGHT: Worked as per Honeycomb #2 (see page 122), but with every other repeat offset. Work the first repeat as written. Work the second repeat offset by 11 stitches—that is, Row 16 starts with p8, and Row 26 starts with picking up 3 stitches from below.

BOTTOM LEFT: Worked as per the top right swatch, but eliminating Rows 17–18.

BOTTOM RIGHT: The wrong side of the top right swatch.

Use the honeycomb technique to create patches of a contrasting color in a variety of fabrics.

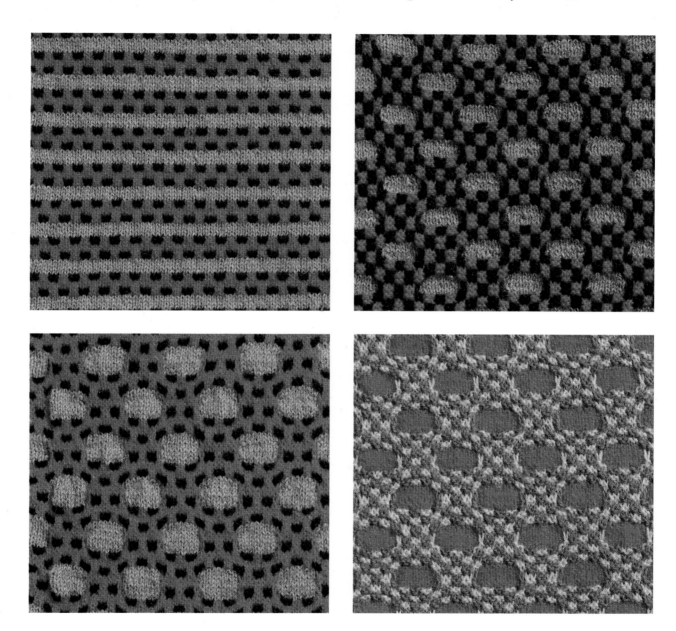

TOP LEFT: The top left swatch shows how the basic fabric is worked—a few plain stockinette rows in a single color alternated with a few rows of a two-color combination stockinette and garter stitch fabric.

TOP RIGHT: A two-color garter stitch fabric is used as the background for patches of plain stockinette in a third color.

BOTTOM LEFT: This fabric is the same as in the top left swatch. When stitches are picked up as per the honeycomb technique, the solid rows of stockinette in the light blue are "broken" and you only see portions of them.

BOTTOM RIGHT: The wrong side of the top right swatch.

CROSSED STITCHES FOR BRAIDED BANDS

I haven't yet delved deeply into the techniques of crossed stitches, surface patterns, and stripes. It is hard to improve upon something that has already been done. I decided to knit braids as narrow bands and then pick up stitches along the long sides and work in stockinette between the horizontal braids. When it's time to join the in-between knitting to the next braid, I pull the stitches to the wrong side and bind off.

Braided Band

You'll need an extra needle or cable needle and a crochet hook. The braid is worked as a band. CO 10 sts.

ROW 1 (WS): P1, k2, p4, k2, p1.

ROW 2 (RS): K2, p1, k4, p1, k2.

ROW 3 (WS): Work as for Row 1.

ROW 4 (RS): K2, p1, slip 2 sts to cable needle and hold in front of work, k2; k2 from cable needle, p1, k2.

Repeat Rows 1–4.

Make 2 of these bands, each about 2–2¾" (5–7 cm) long.

Now pick up stitches along one side of the band between the outer stockinette stitches and the garter stitches, working at gauge for stockinette.

Work in stockinette for desired length, beginning on WS with a purl row.

Pull the stitches through to WS of second band, using a crochet hook.

Bind off.

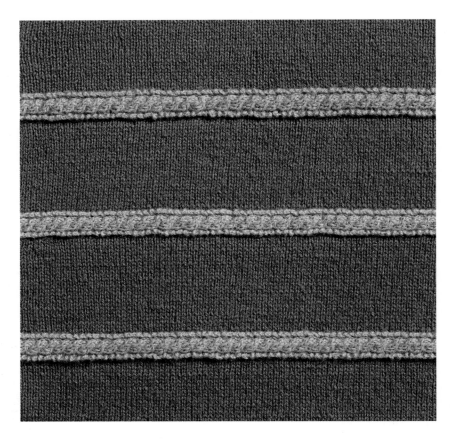

OPPOSITE PAGE: Of course, you can work any stitch pattern between the bands, not just stockinette stitch. In this case, the fabric is a three-color garter stitch check pattern.

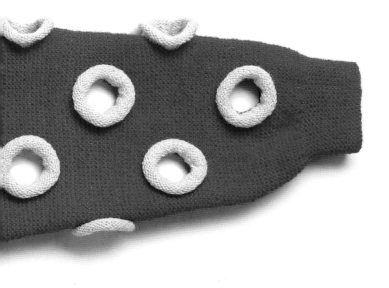

HOLES AND HOLES WITH BORDERS

Lace knitting is not my cup of tea. Lace can be exciting to knit but the result is often too sweet and romantic for my geometrically inclined taste. Nonetheless, twenty years ago I sat down and thought deeply about how I might improve upon the technique. I ultimately came to an alternate approach of making big holes. In general, most of my hole designs are made by binding off, followed by knitting first on one side of the hole and then on the other side. When both sides have been worked, I cast on stitches to bridge the gap between them so that the total stitch count is the same as at the beginning of knitting.

This cardigan is constructed from simple garter stitch pieces worked with an unshaped body and drop sleeve with a simple crew neck following the garment template given on pages 208–209. The lower edges of the body and sleeves are worked on smaller needles to create cuffs. Holes are worked in the garment at regular intervals as per Holes and Holes with Borders #1 (see page 132) and bordered in a contrasting color. Half holes are worked on side and top edges of the body and at the tops of the sleeves so that they line up when the garment is seamed and the borders of those holes worked after the seaming is complete. Stitches are picked up around the neckline, and a facing is worked so that when turned in and sewn down on the inside of the garment, the stockinette side shows.

Holes and Holes with Borders #1

Stitch count: multiple of 40.

5 double-pointed needles needed for rings around the holes.

Work following the chart.

EMPTY SQUARE: 1 stitch and two rows garter stitch.

SHAPE THE HOLE FOLLOWING THE LARGE EMPTY SPACES: Shape bottom edge by binding off. Shape one side and then the other. When both of the sides have been worked, cast on stitches to bridge the gap between them so that the total stitch count is the same as at the beginning of the knitting.

When the fabric with holes has been completed, use the dpn to pick up stitches around the hole. The number of stitches to pick up should match the gauge of the background knitting. Divide the sts over 3 or 4 dpn. Insert the needle tip from RS to WS and bring the border yarn through the stitch loops. Work around in stockinette (knit all rounds). On rnds 3 and 8, increase 4 sts per round. Knit a total of twelve rnds.

Bind off and let knitting roll forward.

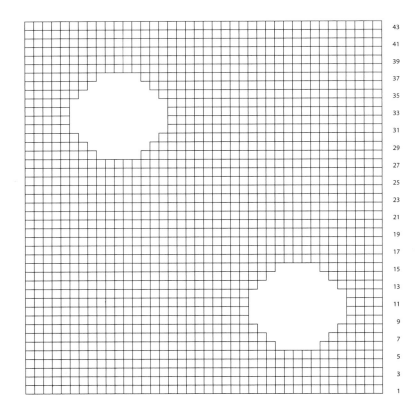

Holes and Holes with Borders #2

Variation.

Follow the chart for the previous hole design but, instead of the hole, work a color spot in intarsia. For information about intarsia, see the Techniques section (page 207).

Pick up and knit sts for the rolled border all around the spot (with RS facing) in the "ditch" between the two colors and work with dpn.

The number of stitches to pick up should match the gauge of the background knitting. Work around in stockinette (knit all rounds). On rnds 3 and 8, increase 4 sts per round. Knit a total of twelve rnds.

Bind off and let knitting roll forward.

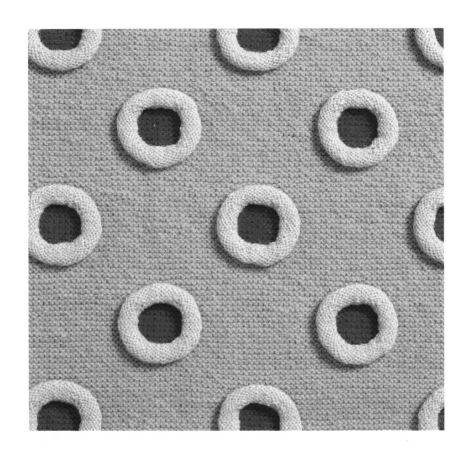

Vary the look by changing the size or shape of the holes or the depth or position of the borders.

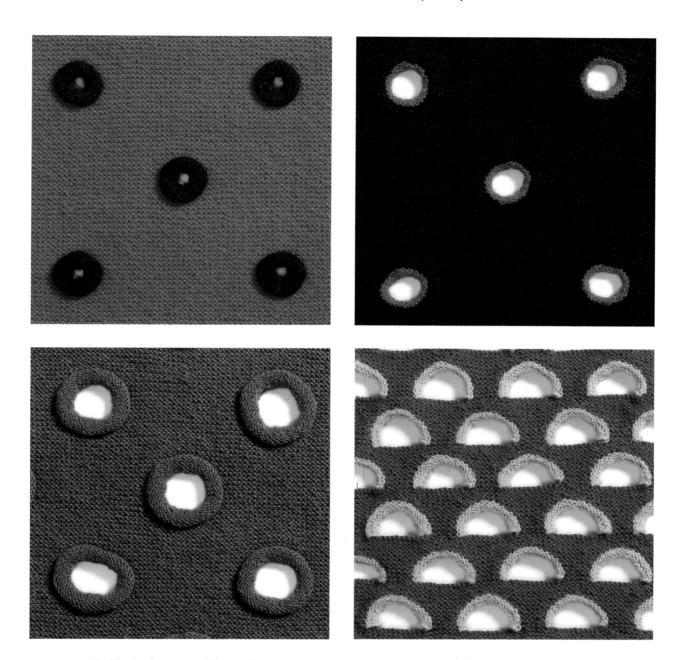

TOP LEFT: A bolder look is created by working more rows of stockinette on the borders.

TOP RIGHT: Or work few rows of stockinette on the border for more open holes.

BOTTOM LEFT: Work larger holes and work the borders in the same color as the background.

BOTTOM RIGHT: A window shape is created by working a straight bind off for the bottom of the hole and curved sides as per the standard hole, with borders only worked on the curved edge.

Holes and Holes with Borders #3

Stitch count: multiple of 16.

ROWS 1–13: Knit (garter stitch).

ROW 14 (RS): *K5, BO 7, k3; rep from *. (4 live sts after BO.)

ROWS 15–26: Work in garter st over the groups of live sts, using separate strands of yarn.

ROW 27 (WS): Knit across first set of sts to the gap and bridge the gap by casting on 7 sts with K-CO (K-CO = *knit 1 st, leaving old st on left needle, twist the new stitch and place on left needle; rep from *); using same strand, knit across rem sts. (Cut all other strands.)

ROW 28 (RS): Knit.

Repeat Rows 2–28.

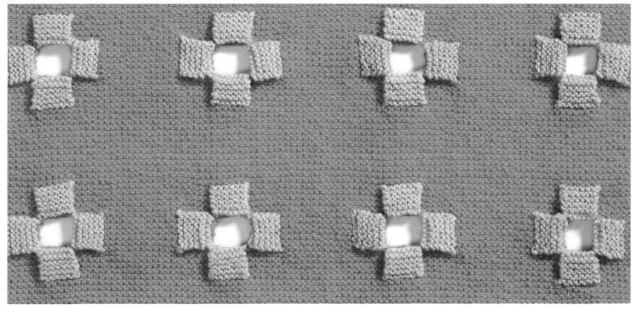

TOP: Work the stitches around the buttonholes in multiple colors using the intarsia method (see page 207). Work strips of garter stitch and sew them down at the corners so that they cross over the holes diagonally.

BOTTOM: Space the holes out further by working more stitches between them and more even rows between a row of holes. Pick up stitches at the edges and work small strips of garter stitch. Fold them to the outside and sew them down.

Use the intarsia method (see page 207) to create crosses in different colors.

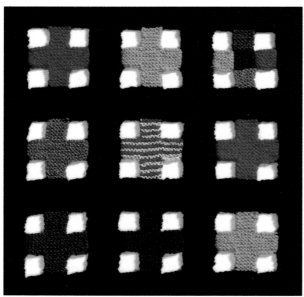

TOP LEFT: After casting off, alternate colors for the separate sections. Cast back on again in the contrasting color. Cast off a second time and continue the separate sections in alternate colors. Cast on the second time in the main color.

TOP RIGHT: Work the center of the crosses in a third color.

BOTTOM LEFT: Work each cross in a different color, or in stripes, or even change colors within the crosses.

BOTTOM RIGHT: Work textural stitches for a different look entirely.

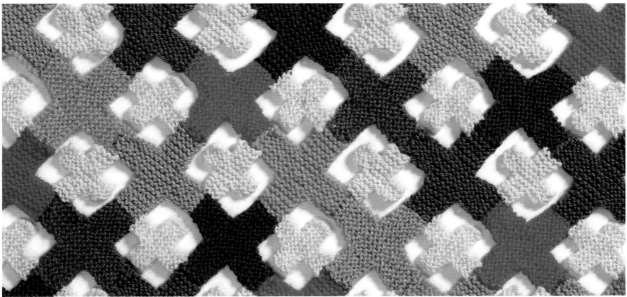

TOP: Rotate the swatches 45 degrees for a totally different look.

BOTTOM: Use different colors for each section to create a pattern of small and large crosses.

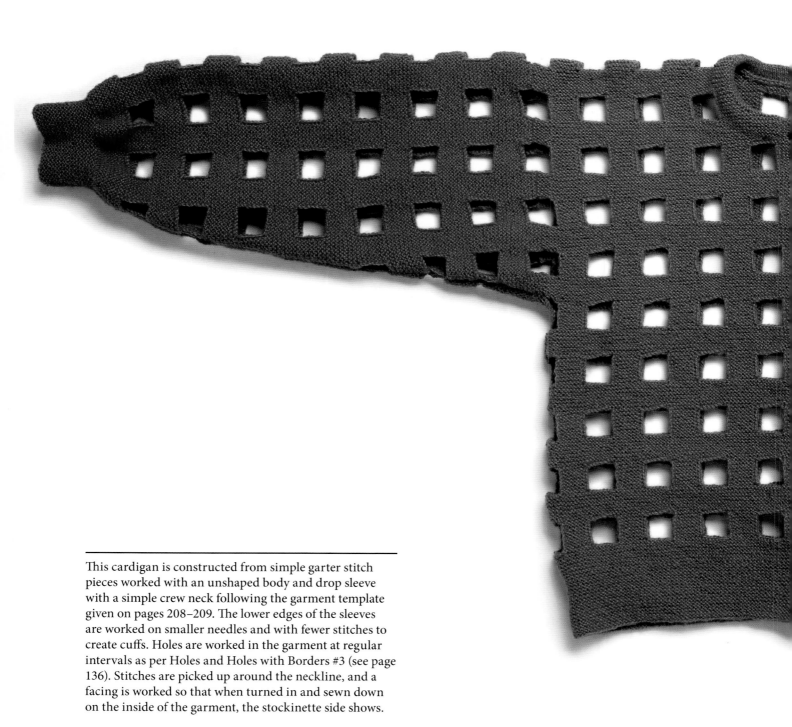

This cardigan is constructed from simple garter stitch pieces worked with an unshaped body and drop sleeve with a simple crew neck following the garment template given on pages 208–209. The lower edges of the sleeves are worked on smaller needles and with fewer stitches to create cuffs. Holes are worked in the garment at regular intervals as per Holes and Holes with Borders #3 (see page 136). Stitches are picked up around the neckline, and a facing is worked so that when turned in and sewn down on the inside of the garment, the stockinette side shows.

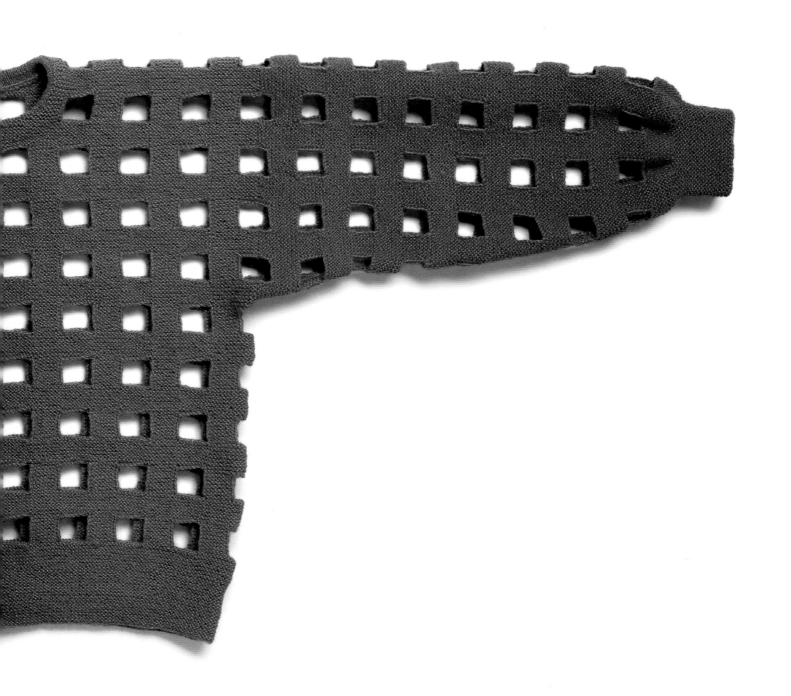

PATTERNS WITH BUTTONHOLES

Another way to make holes in your knitting is to make buttonholes that form patterns, instead of being used to catch buttons. I use the one-row buttonhole so that the holes are less elastic. Even horizontal buttonholes can form patterns. The technique can be decorated with garter or seed stitch, or other stitch patterns that don't roll.

This cardigan is worked with an unshaped body and drop sleeve with a simple crew neck following the garment template given on pages 208–209. The fabric is a two-color variation of Horizontal Buttonhole #1 (see page 144)—Rows 1–6 worked in color 1 and Rows 7–12 worked in a second color, always working the cast on for the buttonholes in the color to be used for the following rows. The reverse stockinette side is facing. Stitches are picked up around the neckline, and a facing is worked with the reverse stockinette side facing so that it rolls down to the inside of the garment.

Horizontal Buttonhole #1

Stitch count: multiple of 10 + 2 edge stitches.

ROWS 1–3: Work in stockinette, beginning on WS with a purl row.

ROW 4 (RS): K1, *k2, make a buttonhole over 7 sts (for buttonhole instructions, see Techniques, page 207); rep from * to last st, k1.

ROWS 5–7: Work in stockinette, beginning on WS with a purl row.

ROW 8 (RS): K1, *make a half-buttonhole over 4 sts, k2, make the other half of the buttonhole over 3 sts*; rep from * to last st, k1.

Repeat Rows 1–8.

VARIATION: Use the reverse stockinette side as the right side.

OPPOSITE PAGE, TOP: RS

OPPOSITE PAGE, BOTTOM: WS

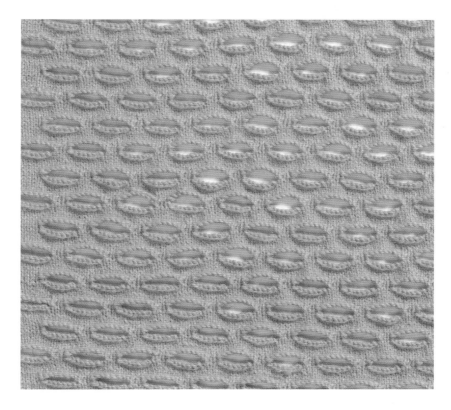

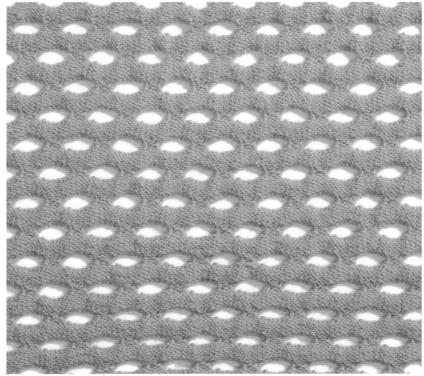

Horizontal Buttonhole #2

Stitch count: multiple of 22.

ROWS 1–5: Work in reverse stockinette, beginning on WS with a knit row.

ROW 6 (RS): *P3, make a buttonhole over 17 sts (for buttonhole instructions, see Techniques, page 207), p1*; rep from * to end.

ROWS 7–11: Work in reverse stockinette, beginning on WS with a knit row.

ROW 12 (RS): *Make a half buttonhole over 9 sts. CO 10 new sts on the empty needle. Move the first st on the left needle to the right needle and bind off the 10th newly cast-on st, p4, work the other half of the buttonhole over 8 sts; rep from *.

(When knitting several wide repeats, cast on the 10 sts at the beginning of the row for the 8 sts at end of repeat.)

One row with several repeats ends with the remaining st at the end bound off with tapestry needle and yarn, and the cast-on is worked with 8 sts.

Repeat Rows 1–12.

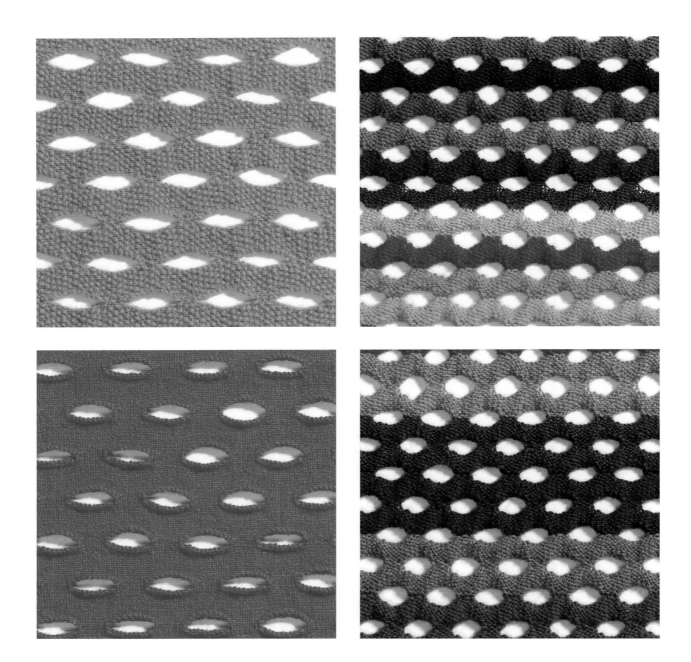

TOP LEFT: Change the look by changing the fabric in which you work the buttonholes. The swatch at the top left is worked in seed stitch.

BOTTOM LEFT: Work more plain rows between the buttonholes for a more solid fabric.

TOP RIGHT: Change color after each set of buttonholes for very impactful stripes.

BOTTOM RIGHT: Work two stripes in each color to change the look of the stripes and emphasize the holes.

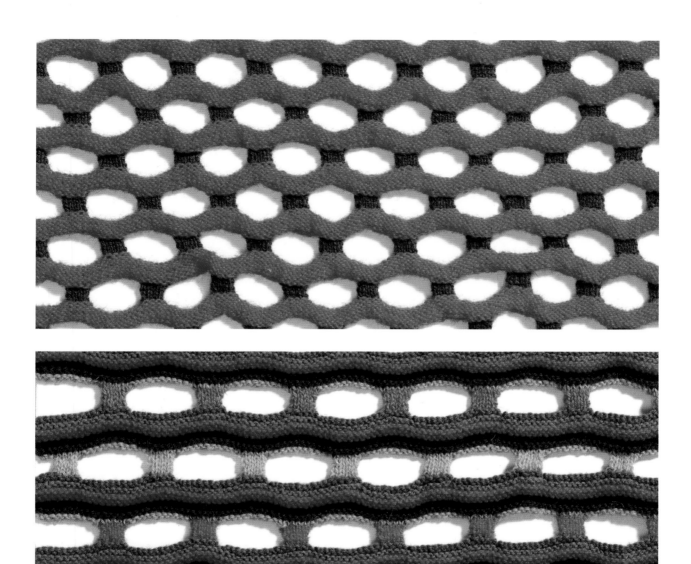

TOP: The fabric is worked in reverse stockinette stitch. Work a few even rows in stockinette stitch on the narrow strips between the buttonholes in a contrasting color.

BOTTOM: Work the complete rows in garter stitch in two-row stripes. Use another color for narrow strips between the buttonholes, worked in stockinette stitch.

This cardigan is worked with an unshaped body and drop sleeve with a simple crew neck following the garment template given on pages 208–209. The fabric is worked as per Horizontal Buttonhole #2 (see page 146), with the reverse stockinette side facing. Stitches are picked up around the neckline, and a facing is worked with the stockinette side facing so that it rolls down to the outside of the garment.

Use two colors to create simpler but equally effective designs.

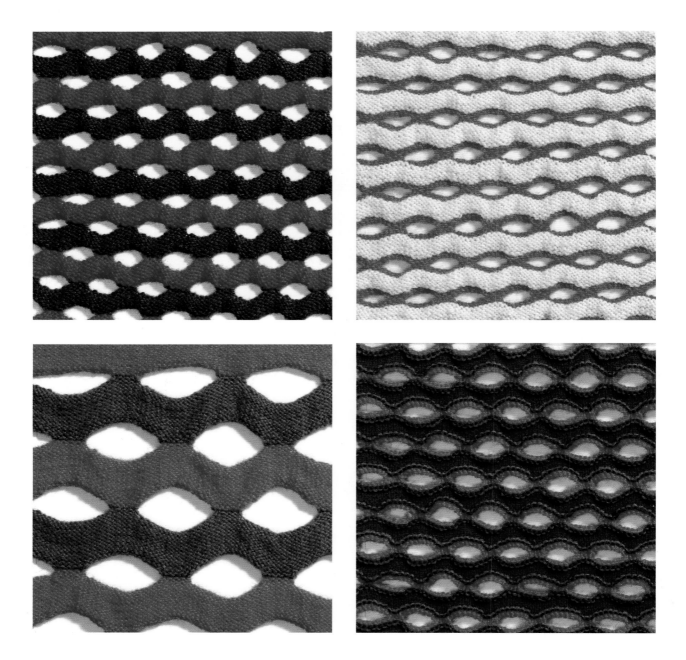

LEFT: Change color after every buttonhole row.

RIGHT: Work the row immediately above and below the buttonholes in a contrasting color.

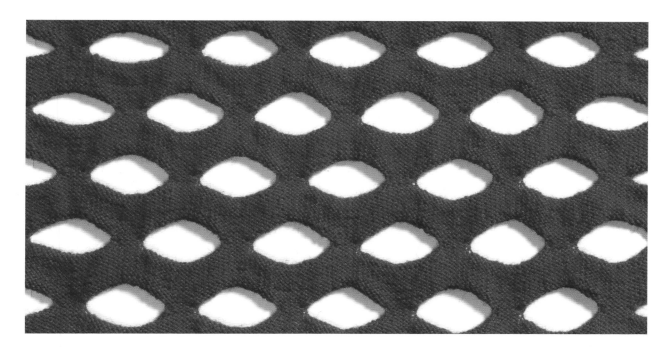

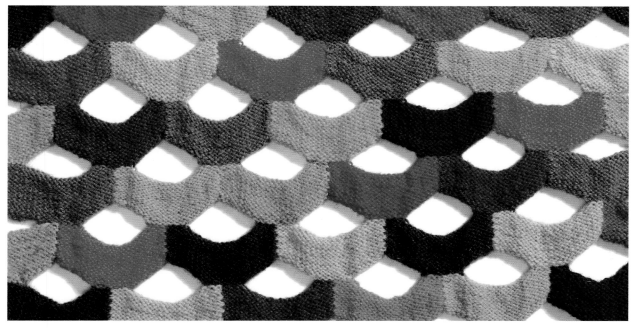

Working with multiple colors can change the look of the fabric entirely. These two swatches are exactly the same, other than the color changes. Use the intarsia method (see page 207) to create blocks of color for each strip of solid fabric. Ensure the buttonholes are centered over each block of color.

Vertical Buttonholes

Stitch count: multiple of 10.

ROW 1 (WS): *K1, p8, k1; rep from *.

ROW 2 (RS): Knit.

Work Rows 1 and 2 three times more and then Row 1 once more.

ROW 10 (RS): K10; turn.

ROW 11 (WS): K1, p8, k1; turn.

Work Rows 10 and 11 five times and then Row 10 once more.

Cut yarn.

Rejoin yarn to next set of live stitches and repeat Rows 10 and 11 as before. When the last repeat of the row is compete, do not cut yarn.

Repeat Rows 1–9.

OPPOSITE PAGE, TOP: RS

OPPOSITE PAGE, BOTTOM: WS

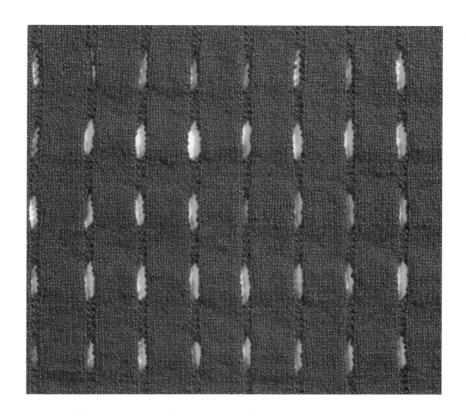

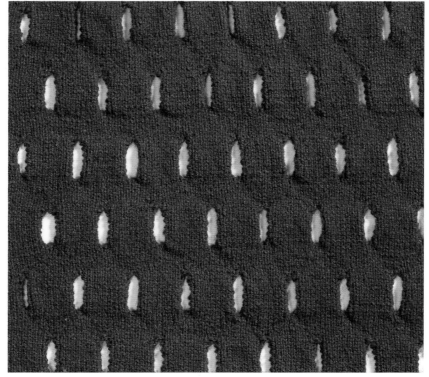

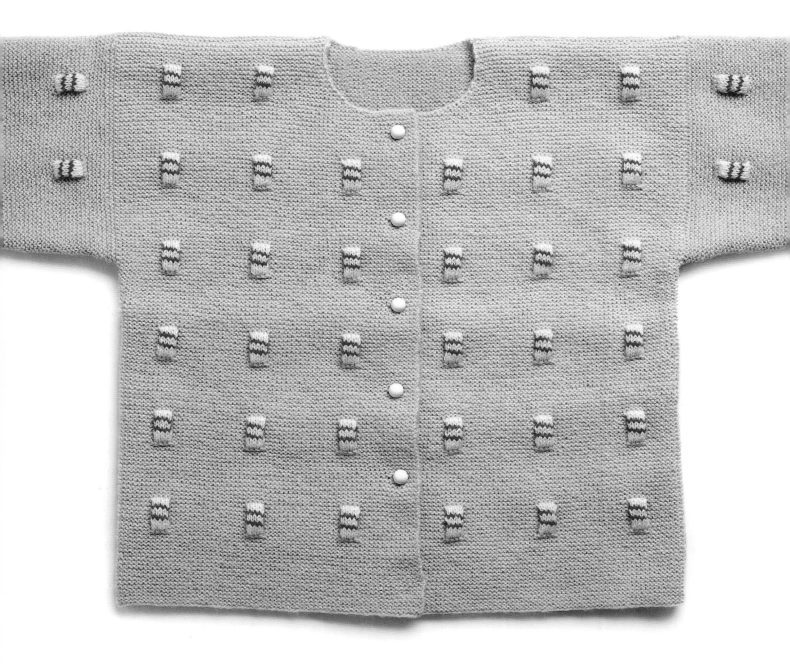

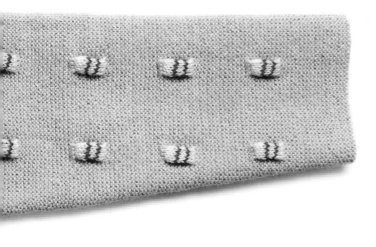

SURFACE MOTIFS OVER BACKGROUND KNITTING 1

You have a great deal of freedom when it comes to placing motifs on the surface of your knitting. These shapes provide a more prominent relief structure. If I'm knitting a garment with motifs that will lie on top of the surface (which I plan before beginning), I leave the stitches for the relief motif on a stitch holder, turn the knitting and pick up the same number of stitches from the previous row. I turn the knitting again and continue the background knitting until it matches the length that the relief motifs will be. Now I can knit the motifs (using two extra needles) and, when the background and pattern knitting meet, I can knit them together. You can also pick up stitches on an already finished piece of knitting, knit the pattern shapes, pull the stitches to the wrong side, and bind them off.

This cardigan is constructed from simple garter stitch pieces worked with an unshaped body and drop sleeve with a simple crew neck following the garment template given on pages 208–209. Stockinette stitch relief blocks worked in stripes of two colors are attached at regular intervals.

Surface Motifs over Background Knitting 1: #1

Stitch count: multiple of 10.

You'll need 4 needles, including 2 dpn for the relief blocks. Youll also need some stitch holders.

ROW 1 (WS): Knit.

ROW 2 (RS): *K5, place 5 sts on a holder; turn work and pick up 5 sts from previous row; turn and k5; rep from *.

ROWS 3–11: Knit all rows (garter stitch).

ROW 12 (RS): *K5, slip 5 sts from holder to the third needle and, with a new yarn strand and the fourth needle, k1f&b in each st—10 sts. For all rows of the block, work *k1, sl 1 wyf; rep from *. The block is finished when it is the same length as the background knitting.

Cut yarn and move it to the WS while, *at the same time,* positioning the needle so it lies parallel to background knitting. (K 1 st from the front needle and 1 st from the back needle together through the back loop) 5 times.

ROW 13 (WS): Knit.

ROW 14 (RS): *Place 5 sts on a holder; turn work and pick up 5 sts from previous row; turn work, k10; rep from *.

ROWS 15–23: Knit all rows.

ROW 24 (RS): Slip 5 sts from holder to a third needle and, with a new yarn strand and the fourth needle, k1f&b in each st—10 sts. For all rows of the block, work *k1, sl 1 wyf; rep from *. The block is finished when it is the same length as the background knitting.

Cut yarn and move it to the WS while, *at the same time,* positioning the needle so it lies parallel to background knitting. (K 1 st from the front needle and 1 st from the back needle together through the back loop) 5 times, k5; rep from *.

Repeat Rows 1–24.

Relief blocks are equally effective worked against a background of garter stitch.

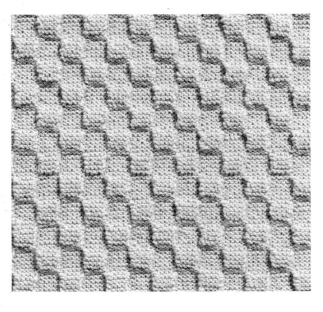

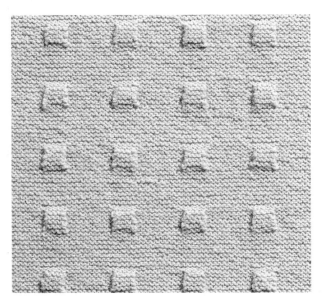

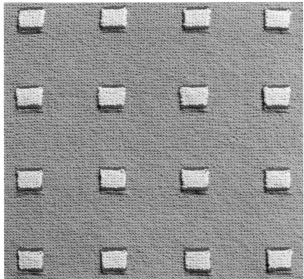

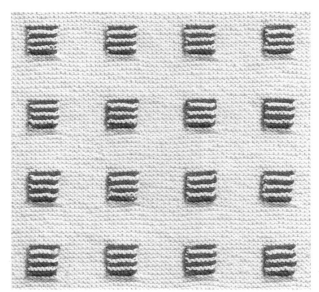

TOP LEFT: Five-stitch five-ridge blocks placed in a checkerboard pattern on a background of garter stitch, worked in a single color.

TOP RIGHT: Place the blocks further apart for more impact.

BOTTOM: Work relief blocks in stripes of contrasting colors.

OPPOSITE PAGE: The fabric for this garment is created using the basic method of Surface Motifs over Background Knitting 1: #2 (see page 162), but with larger triangles oriented the other way around: the triangle starts with a single stitch and increases to 13 stitches. The neckline is square, created with simple bind-offs for the full width of the neckline.

Surface Motifs over Background Knitting 1: #2

Stitch count: multiple of 8.

You'll need 4 needles, including 2 dpn for the relief blocks. You'll also need some stitch holders.

ROW 1 (WS): Knit.

ROW 2 (RS): *K1, k7, place 7 sts on a holder; turn work and pick up 7 sts from previous row; turn and k7; rep from *.

ROWS 3–13: Knit all rows (garter stitch).

ROW 14 (RS): *K4, place 4 sts on a holder; turn work and pick up 4 sts from previous row; turn work, k4, move the 7 sts from holder to the third needle and with a new strand of yarn, work:

Triangle

ROWS 1–4: Knit.

ROW 5 (RS): K2tog, k3, k2tog tbl.

ROWS 6–8: Knit.

ROW 9 (RS): K2tog, k1, k2tog tbl.

ROWS 10–12: Knit.

ROW 13 (RS): Sl 1 wyb, k2tog, psso.

ROW 14 (WS): Knit.

Knit remaining st of triangle together with next st on left needle. K3, place 3 sts on a holder; turn work and pick up 3 sts from previous row; turn work, k3.

ROWS 15–25: Knit (garter stitch).

ROW 26: *Place 4 sts from holder onto third needle and work.

Half triangle with decreases on left side

ROWS 1–4: Knit.

ROW 5 (RS): K2, k2tog tbl.

ROWS 6–8: Knit.

ROW 9 (RS): K1, k2tog tbl.

ROWS 10–12: Knit.

ROW 13 (RS): K2tog tbl.

ROW 14 (WS): Knit.

Knit remaining st of half triangle together with first st on left needle. K7, place 7 sts on a holder; turn work and pick up 7 sts from previous row; turn work, k7; rep from *. *Note:* When working with more than 1 repeat of 8 sts, work across the row as follows: move the 7 sts from holder onto the third needle, knit a TRIANGLE and then join it to the background knitting as on Row 14.

After all repeats are worked, the row ends with a half triangle: move 3 sts from holder to a needle and work them as follows:

Half triangle with decreases on right side

ROWS 1–4: Knit.

ROW 5 (RS): K2tog, k1.

ROWS 6–8: Knit.

ROW 9 (RS): K2tog.

ROW 10 (WS): Knit.

Cut yarn and pull tail through last stitch; sew triangle tip to background knitting.

Repeat Rows 3–26.

Work relief blocks in garter stitch as per Surface Motifs Over Background Knitting 1: #3 (see page 166), but without twisting the strips.

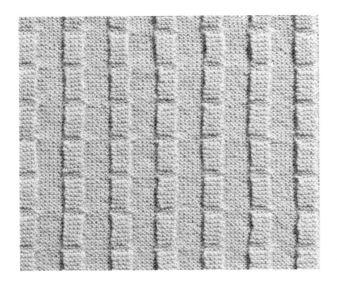 

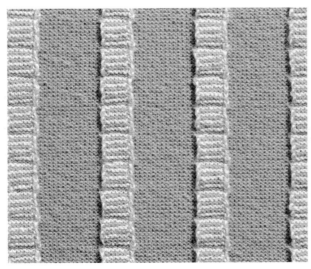 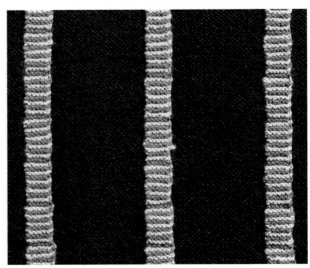

TOP LEFT: Use a single color for both the background and the relief blocks.

TOP RIGHT: Use a single color for both the background and the relief blocks and work a single WS row in a contrasting color to create a line between the rows of blocks.

BOTTOM LEFT: Work stripes with a contrasting color on the blocks, slipping the first stitch of every row to create a more prominent edge to the block.

Use the contrasting color to knit the stitches of the block together with the background stitches.

BOTTOM RIGHT: The blocks are striped with two contrasting colors, but unlike the bottom left swatch, the first stitch of every row is worked as per the rest of the row. Use one of the contrasting colors to knit the stitches of the block together with the background stitches.

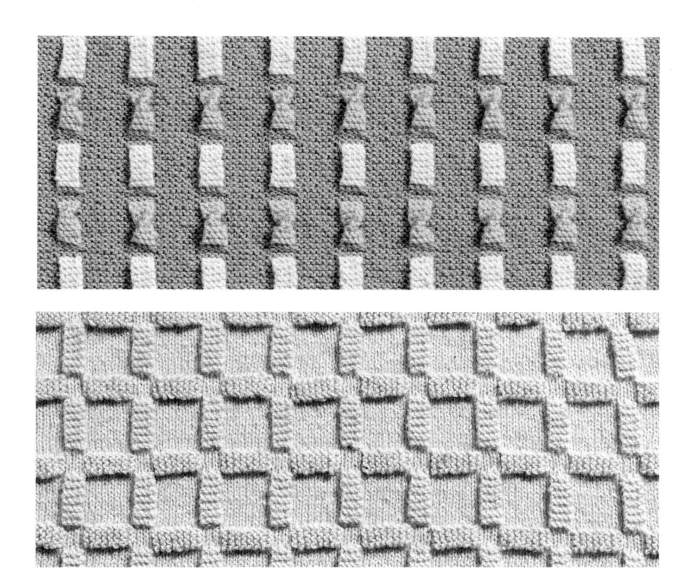

TOP: Alternate rows of untwisted and twisted garter stitch relief blocks as per Surface Motifs Over Background Knitting 1: #3, separated by two ridges of garter stitch.

BOTTOM: Work rows of untwisted garter stitch relief blocks as per Surface Motifs Over Background Knitting 1: #3 in the same color as the background, separated by a few rows of stockinette stitch. Between the rows of relief blocks, work garter stitch blocks lying perpendicularly to the fabric by picking up stitch between two columns of stitches in the background fabric. Anchor the perpendicular blocks by binding them off and sewing them down.

Surface Motifs over Background Knitting 1: #3

Stitch count: multiple of 12.

A second color is used for the spirals that hover over the surface of the background knitting in the main color. You'll need 4 needles, including 2 dpn for the spiral strips. You'll also need some stitch holders. Because the yarn follows the spiral as you work, you'll need a separate ball of yarn for each spiral. To avoid dealing with multiple balls of yarn tangling, just use a free-hanging strand of yarn for each spiral. That way you can easily pull the strands apart if necessary.

ROW 1 (WS): Knit.

ROW 2 (RS): *K4, place 4 sts on a holder; turn work, pick up 4 sts from previous row; turn work, k8; rep from *.

Note: When working the lengthwise repeats and using two colors, pick up stitches in the same color as background knitting.

ROWS 3–21: Knit all rows (garter stitch).

ROW 22 (RS): *K4, move 4 sts on holder to the third needle and, with color 2, knit twenty-one rows. Do not cut yarn. Make a half turn in the strip and hold the needle parallel to the background knitting. Join the strip to the background: Using color 2, knit 1 st from the front needle together with 1 st from back needle 4 times, k4*; rep from *.

Repeat Rows 1–22. When repeating the pattern, work the spiral stitches on Row 1 with color 2, which leaves the yarn on the RS.

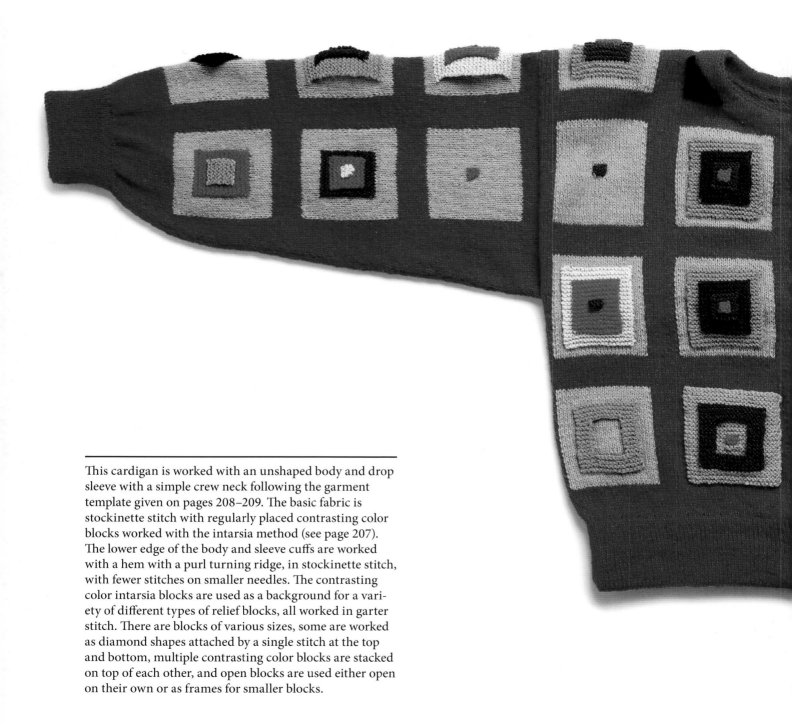

This cardigan is worked with an unshaped body and drop sleeve with a simple crew neck following the garment template given on pages 208–209. The basic fabric is stockinette stitch with regularly placed contrasting color blocks worked with the intarsia method (see page 207). The lower edge of the body and sleeve cuffs are worked with a hem with a purl turning ridge, in stockinette stitch, with fewer stitches on smaller needles. The contrasting color intarsia blocks are used as a background for a variety of different types of relief blocks, all worked in garter stitch. There are blocks of various sizes, some are worked as diamond shapes attached by a single stitch at the top and bottom, multiple contrasting color blocks are stacked on top of each other, and open blocks are used either open on their own or as frames for smaller blocks.

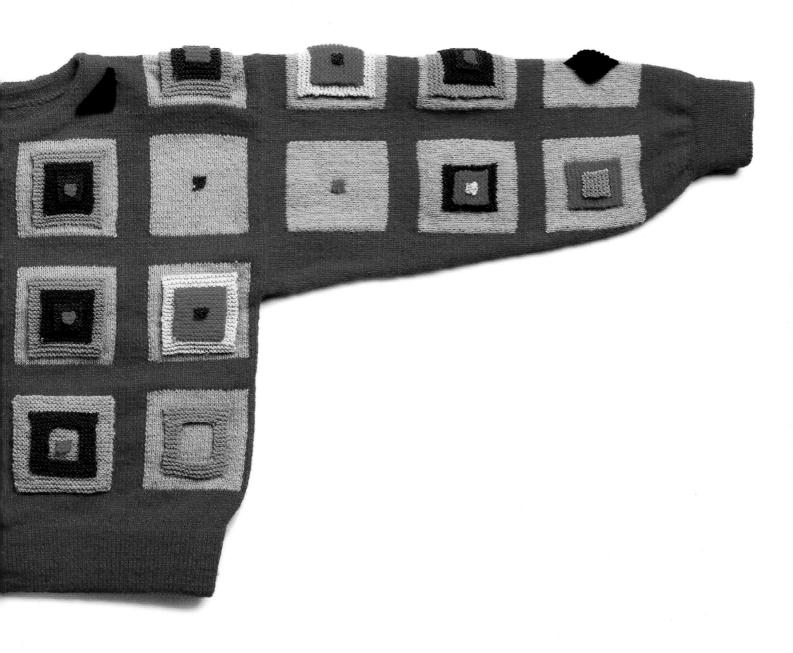

Create a circular relief block by working increases at each end of the block on the first few rows, working even, and then decreasing again at the ends of the block back to the original number of stitches.

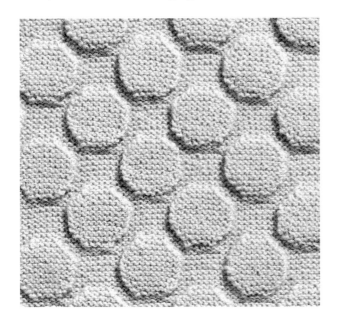 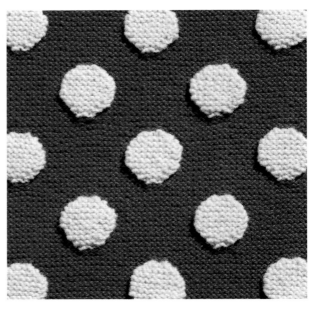

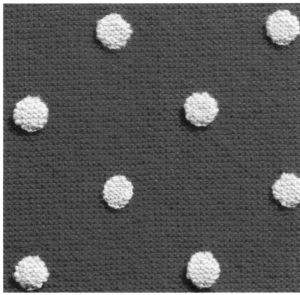 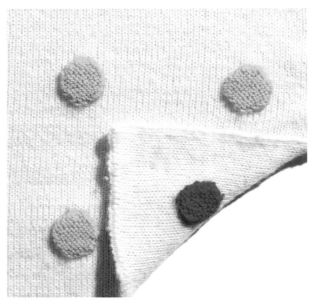

TOP LEFT: Work them in the same color as the background, spaced closely on the background fabric.

TOP RIGHT: Work them in a contrasting color and space them out.

BOTTOM LEFT: Work smaller circular blocks spaced further apart for a polka dot effect.

BOTTOM RIGHT: Place the blocks in a square pattern and work them on different colors on the two sides of two-sided fabric.

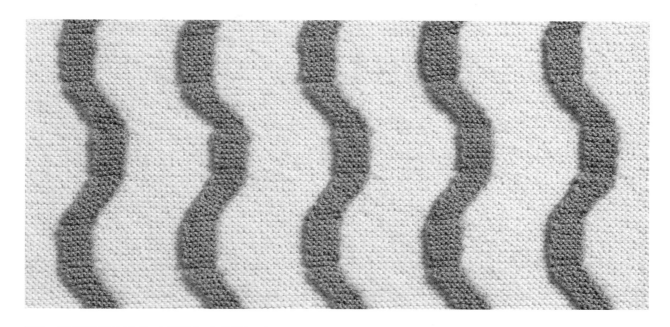

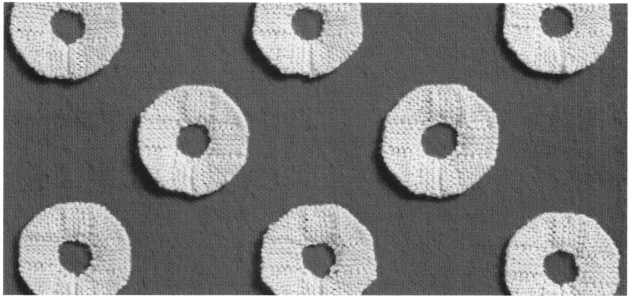

TOP: Work garter stitch relief blocks as per Surface Motifs Over Background Knitting 1: #3 (see page 166), without twisting. On every alternate join, move the block over, joining it to stitches before or after the previous join.

BOTTOM: Work rings as per Shortened and Lengthened Rows #1 (see page 196), picking up the starting stitches from the background. To close up the ring, work the final stitches together with the background stitches.

SURFACE MOTIFS OVER BACKGROUND KNITTING 2

Another option for working surface motifs that float over the background knitting is to simply make two separate pieces of knitting. In that case, the relief motifs are not connected along the lower edge.

Surface Motifs over Background Knitting 2: #1

Stitch count: any number.

BACKGROUND KNITTING, ROWS 1–11: Work in stockinette, beginning on WS with a purl row.

FLOATING WELT: Use same stitch count as for background knitting.

ROWS 1–7: Work in stockinette, beginning on WS with a knit row.

Hold both pieces of knitting parallel and join by knitting together 1 st from front needle and 1 st from back needle. The floating welt has the reverse stockinette side facing outward and rolls inward.

Repeat from beginning to end of pattern above.

Surface Motifs over Background Knitting 2: #2

Stitch count: multiple of 8.

BACKGROUND KNITTING: Work 19 rows in stockinette, beginning on WS with a purl row.

FLOATING RECTANGLES: CO 5 sts and work seventeen rows in garter stitch. Make some rectangles a single color and others striped. Vary the colors and stripes.

*K2, hold both needles parallel and (knit together 1 st from front needle and 1 st from back needle) 5 times, k1; rep from *.

Repeat from beginning to end of pattern above.

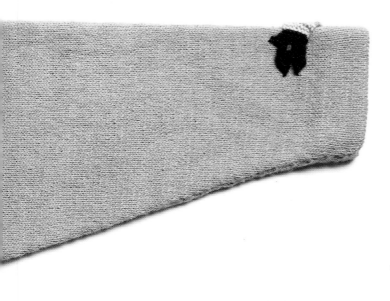

SURFACE MOTIFS OVER BACKGROUND KNITTING 3

These collared sweaters are embellished with floating surface patterns that are even more free-form than the previous examples. Sometimes I had to sleep on an idea before I could decide on the precise arrangement. At the beginning of the 1990s, the Hälsingland Museum in Hudiksvall, Sweden, had a huge exhibition of folk art. A number of harness hooks (carved in wood to decorate horse harnesses) hung from the ceiling like a flock of birds. They were so fascinating and, of course, inspiring, with their lovely carvings, painted shapes, and figures. That's exactly where the idea for these sweater collars was born.

These cardigans are worked with an unshaped body and a modified drop sleeve with a simple crew neck following the garment template given on pages 208–209. The lower edge of the body and sleeve cuffs are worked with a hem with a purl turning ridge, in stockinette stitch. Various decorative elements are worked separately and sewn onto the garments. The black-and-white snakes around the neck are worked in garter stitch, the yellow serpents are created from wide strips of garter stitch with narrower strips of stockinette stitch (with stitches worked in black) sewn on top. The round patches are worked in garter stitch, with a long strip of stockinette stitch sewn down around the edges. All the creatures' heads are worked in garter stitch. Garter stitch diamond shapes are sewn down at the back of the neck, to create a kerchief effect.

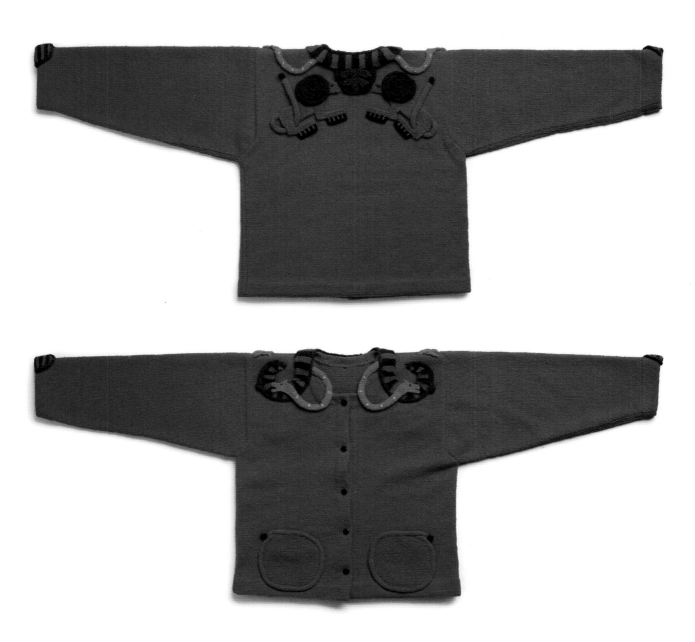

This cardigan is worked with an unshaped body and a modified drop sleeve with a simple crew neck following the garment template given on pages 208–209. The lower edge of the body and sleeve cuffs are worked with a hem with a purl turning ridge, in stockinette stitch. Various decorative elements are worked separately and sewn onto the garment. Both the red and green striped and solid blue strips around the neck are worked in garter stitch. A red serpent is created from a narrow strip of stockinette stitch (with stitches worked in yellow), with a garter stitch head. The round patches are worked in garter stitch, with a long strip of stockinette stitch sewn down around the edges. The creatures on the back are worked in garter stitch with narrow stockinette stitch cords for the ears and the tails. Garter stitch patches are worked and sewn between the two creatures.

KNITTING IN DIFFERENT DIRECTIONS

This technique is derived from entrelac, an old style of knitting with diagonal blocks. One row of blocks is made first and then a new row of blocks is picked up and worked in the opposite direction. At the same time, the new block is joined to a block on the previous row. I've adapted that concept to produce right-angled cables: one narrow and loose and the other wide and tight.

Knitting in Different Directions #1

BAND 1: CO 8 sts. Work 48 rows in garter stitch; do not bind off. Place sts on a holder.

BAND 2: Pick up and knit 8 sts, 1 st in each "knot" of WS row, along left side of Band 1, beginning 8 WS rows up. Knit 48 rows in garter stitch; do not bind off.

BAND 3: CO 8 sts on same needle as Band 2 sts sit on and knit 16 rows in garter st with the new sts. Knit the last st on Row 17 together with the first st on Band 2. Turn work and slip first st. Continue joining sts until the 8 sts of Band 2 have been eliminated. Knit sixteen rows garter st; do not bind off; place sts on a holder.

BAND 4: Work as for Band 2, but pick up and knit sts along left side of Band 3.

BAND 5: Work as for Band 3, joining sts to Band 4.

BAND 6: CO 8 sts. Move sts of Band 1 to a second needle and knit fifteen rows garter st on the new sts. Knit the last st on Row 16 together with nearest st on Band 1. Knit sts together through back loops. When the 8 sts of Band 1 are eliminated, knit seventeen rows garter st. Do not bind off. Place sts on a holder.

BAND 7: Using same needle holding the sts for Band 6, pick up and knit 8 sts along top edge of Band 2. Work as for Band 3, attaching it to Band 6. BO across band if the piece ends on this tier.

BAND 8: Move sts of Band 3 to a needle. Pick up and knit 8 sts along left edge of Band 7 with the second needle. Work as for Band 6, attaching it to Band 3.

BAND 9: Using same needle holding sts of Band 8, pick up and knit 8 sts along top edge of Band 4. Work as for Band 3, attaching it to Band 8. BO across band if the piece ends on this tier.

BAND 10: Move sts of Band 5 to a needle. Pick up and knit 8 sts along left side of Band 9 with the second needle. Work as for Band 6, attaching it to Band 5. BO across band if it is the last one of the left edge.

To fill in the knitting and balance the outer edges, pick up and knit 8 sts at each place marked "11" on the drawing below. Knit sixteen rows for each segment and then BO.

The bands can be knit in different colors.

For example, so that the piece will look more clearly like a lattice, knit the odd-numbered bands with one color and the even-numbered bands with another color.

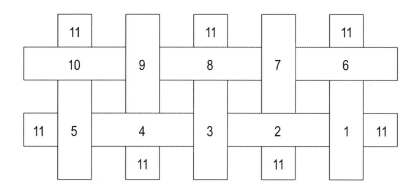

Knitting in Different Directions #2

Any number of colors. Since the rows are short, use dpn. You'll also need some stitch holders. The instructions below are for the swatch shown in the drawing.

CROSSES 1 AND 2: Work each separately. CO 6 sts and knit 11 rows in garter st. K-CO 6 sts (at right) and k12. K-CO 6 sts for left leg. Knit 11 rows.

BO 6 sts, k11, BO 6, k5.

Knit 11 rows over remaining 6 sts. Place these sts on a holder (but BO Cross 2). Cut yarn.

CROSS 3: Pick up and knit 6 sts along top left leg of Cross 2. Work as for Cross 1; before casting on second set of 6 sts, move sts of Cross 1 from holder to the empty needle, then complete CO. K18, turn. K17, knit the 18th st together with first st of Cross 1 tbl. Continue joining the same way until eleven rows have been knit. BO 6 sts, at right side. K10 and work the last k2tog tbl. BO 6 sts. Knit eleven rows over remaining 6 sts. Place sts on a holder and cut yarn.

CROSS 4: CO and work as for Cross 1. Move sts of Cross 3 to the empty needle before casting on the first set of 6 sts. Continue with the second cast on and then join with Crosses 3 and 4 as before. Continue to work as for Cross 1.

CROSS 5: Pick up and knit 6 sts along top right leg of Cross 3. Work as for Cross 1. BO when Cross is complete.

So that the piece will have straight edges, work the fill-in segments. See diagram for guide to their locations.

FILL-IN 6 (IT IS WORKED IN THE "WRONG" DIRECTION BUT THAT MAKES IT EASIER): Pick up and knit 6 sts. Knit 1 row. BO 1 st at beginning of each row until no sts remain.

FILL-IN 7: Pick up and knit 6 sts. Knit 1 row, BO 1 st. Continue knitting and binding off 1 st along one side until no sts remain.

FILL-IN 8: Pick up and knit 6 sts. BO 1. Continue knitting and binding off 1 st along one side until no sts remain.

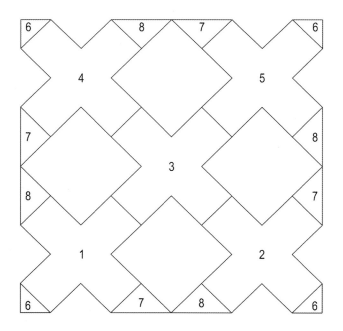

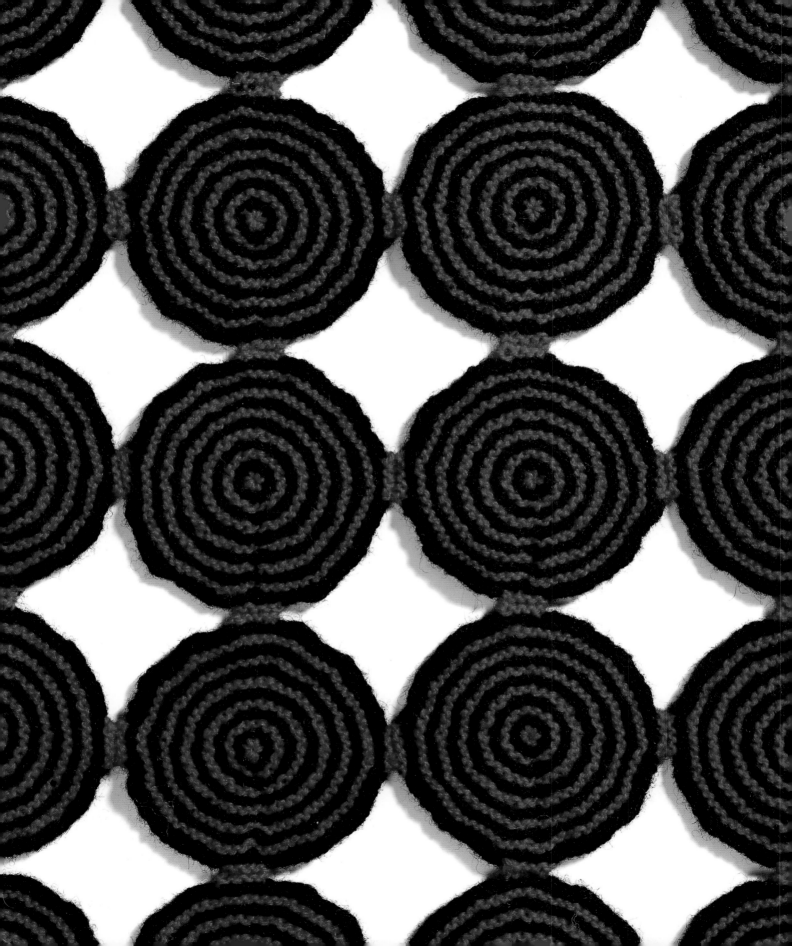

JOINING STITCHES IN SUCCESSION

If you want to make knitted shapes by joining, try knitting circles. Of course, it might be simpler to knit circles with double-pointed needles. However, I prefer to knit them back and forth. After casting on 84 stitches, I work back and forth, shaping the piece into a circle until 7 stitches remain. Then I seam the circle from the center to the outer edge.

Joining Stitches in Succession

Worked back and forth in garter stitch with two colors.
With color 1, CO 84 sts.

ROW 1 (WS): With color 1, knit.

ROW 2 (RS): *With color 2, k4, k2tog; rep from *.

ROW 3 (WS): With color 2, knit.

ROWS 4 AND 5: With color 1, knit.

ROW 6 (RS): *With color 2, k3, k2tog; rep from *.

ROW 7 (WS): With color 2, knit.

ROWS 8 AND 9: With color 1, knit.

ROW 10 (RS): *With color 2, k2, k2tog; rep from *.

ROW 11 (WS): With color 2, knit.

ROWS 12 AND 13: With color 1, knit.

ROW 14 (RS): *With color 2, k1, k2tog; rep from *.

ROW 15 (WS): With color 2, knit.

ROWS 16 AND 17: With color 1, knit.

ROW 18: *With color 2, k2tog; rep from *.

ROW 19 (WS): With color 2, knit.

ROWS 20 AND 21: With color 1, knit.

ROW 22 (RS): *With color 2, k2tog; rep from *.

Now 7 sts remain. Cut yarn. Thread yarn tail into tapestry needle and pull tail through rem 7 sts, pull tight. Now sew the piece into a circle.

Make several circles and sew or knit them together.

To knit the circles together, pick up and knit a few stitches (7, for example) at each of the four "compass points." Knit a few rows in garter stitch on each.

When the circles meet, join them with three-needle bind off, holding pieces RS facing RS and needles parallel.

The circles can also be knit in the round. CO 84 sts, divide over dpn. Follow the instructions above but purl all the odd-numbered rounds.

VERTICAL INCREASES AND DECREASES

The starting point for this pattern is a technique that makes vertical stripes when the stitches are pulled into the diagonal because of the sequencing of increases and decreases. The lower edge becomes triangular. I have combined this chevron pattern with intarsia knitting and shaped the triangles by alternately increasing and decreasing.

191

Vertical Increases and Decreases

Stitch count: multiple of 14 + 1.

You'll need an extra needle. The piece is worked with three colors in intarsia (see page 207). Colors 2 and 3 are used for two-color stranded knitting. When changing to/from the single color segments, hold colors 2 and 3 together to twist them around color 1.

CO with color 1.

With color 1, purl 1 row. Do not repeat this setup row.

ROW 1 (RS): *With color 1, k7. With color 2, k1. With color 1, k6; rep from * to last st, k1.

ROW 2 (WS): With color 1, p1, *p6. With color 2, p1. With color 1, p7*.

ROW 3 (RS): *With color 1, k1, k2tog, k4. With color 2, increase 1 st with backward loop (bring yarn over right needle from WS of knitting to RS), k1, inc 1. With color 1, k4, k2tog tbl; rep from * to last st, k1.

ROW 4 AND ALL EVEN-NUMBERED ROWS THROUGH ROW 28 (WS): Purl, working colors as they lie.

ROW 5 (RS): *With color 1, k1, k2tog, k3. With color 2, k1. With color 3, inc 1. With color 2, k1. With color 3, inc 1. With color 2, k1. With color 1, k3, k2tog tbl; rep from * to last st, k1.

ROW 7 (RS): *With color 1, k1, k2tog, k2. With color 2, k1. With color 3, k1. With color 2, inc 1, k1, inc 1. With color 3, k1. With color 2, k1. With color 1, k2, k2tog tbl; rep from * to last st, k1.

ROW 9 (RS): *With color 1, k1, k2tog, k1. With color 2, k1. With color 3, k1. With color 2, k1. With color 3, inc 1. With color 2, k1. With color 3, inc 1. With color 2, k1. With color 3, k1. With color 2, k1. With color 1, k1, k2tog tbl; rep from * to last st, k1.

ROW 11 (RS): *With color 1, k1, k2tog. With color 2, k1. With color 3, k1. With color 2, k1. With color 3, k1. With color 2, inc 1, k1, inc 1. With color 3, k1. With color 2, k1. With color 3, k1. With color 2, k1. With color 1, k2tog tbl; rep from * to last st, k1.

ROW 13 (RS): With color 1, k2tog tbl. *With color 2, k1. With color 3, k1. With color 2, k1. With color 3, k1. With color 2, k1. With color 3, inc 1. With color 2, k1. With color 3, inc 1. With color 2, k1. With color 3, k1. With color 2, k1. With color 3, k1. With color 2, k1. With color 1, s2kp2o. Move st from extra to left needle and k2tog tbl. Continue from *, working final

decrease as k2tog.

ROW 15 (RS): *With color 2, k1. With color 1, k13*. With color 2, k1.

ROW 17 (RS): *With color 2, k1, inc 1. With color 1, k4, k2tog tbl, k1, k2tog, k4. With color 2, inc 1*; rep from * to last st k1.

ROW 19 (RS): *With color 2, k1. With color 3, inc 1. With color 2, k1. With color 1, k3, k2tog tbl, k1, k2tog, k3. With color 2, k1. With color 3, inc 1; rep from * to last st. With color 2, k1.

ROW 21 (RS): *With color 2, k1, inc 1. With color 3, k1. With color 2, k1. With color 1, k2, k2tog tbl, k1, k2tog, k2. With color 2, k1. With color 3, k1. With color 2, inc 1; rep from * to last st, With color 2, k1.

ROW 23 (RS): *With color 2, k1. With color 3, inc 1. With color 2, k1. With color 3, k1. With color 2, k1. With color 1, k1, k2tog tbl, k1, k2tog, k1. With color 2, k1. With color 3, k1. With color 2, k1. With color 3, inc 1; rep from * to last st. With color 2, k1.

ROW 25 (RS): *With color 2, k1, inc 1. With color 3, k1. With color 2, k1. With color 3, k1. With color 2, k1. With color 1, k2tog tbl, k1, k2tog. With color 2, k1. With color 3, k1. With color 2, k1. With color 3, k1. With color 2, inc 1; rep from * to last st, with color 2, k1k1.

ROW 27 (RS): *With color 2, k1. With color 3, inc 1. With color 2, k1. With color 3, k1. With color 2, k1. With color 3, k1. With color 2, k1, s2kp2o. With color 2, k1. With color 3, k1. With color 2, k1. With color 3, k1. With color 2, k1. With color 3, inc 1; rep from * to last st. With color 2, k1.

ROW 28 (WS): Purl, working colors as they lie.

Repeat Rows 1–28.

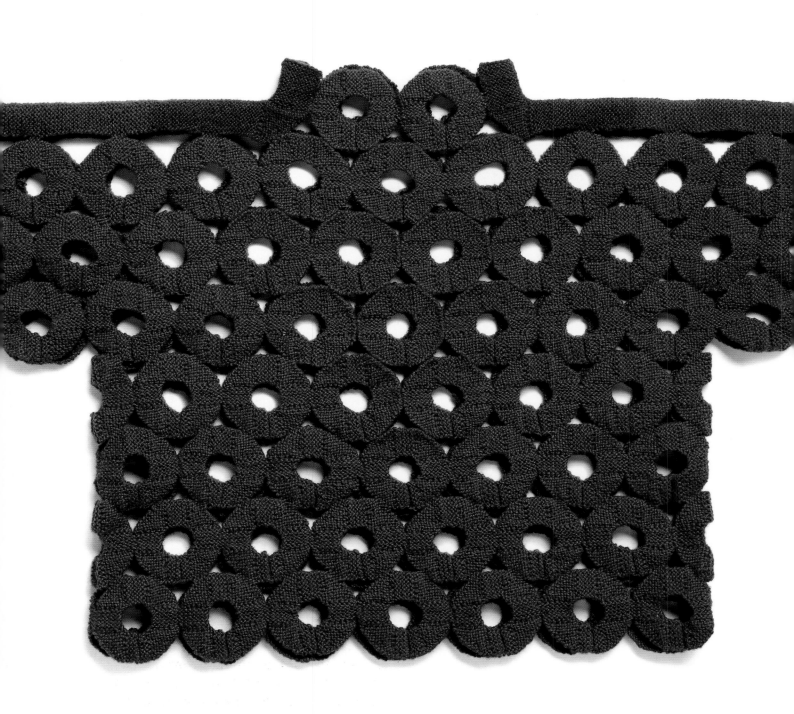

SHORTENED AND LENGTHENED ROWS

The shortened and lengthened rows of the rings make the knitting bend. You begin at the outer edge of the ring so that the outer circumference gradually becomes larger than the inner. The rings are each knitted separately and then are knitted together by picking up stitches from two rings and joining them with three-needle bind off at the same time. The very free forms shown in this section also have shortened and lengthened rows as the basic technique, but, in addition, include casting on and binding off as part of the shaping process. I have worked the technique as the whim took me, picking up and joining shapes one after the other.

Shortened and Lengthened Rows #1

You'll need an extra needle.
CO 7 sts.

ROWS 1–6: K7.

ROW 7 (RS): K2, turn.

ROW 8 (WS): Sl 1 wyb, k1.

ROW 9 (RS): K3, turn.

ROW 10 (WS): Sl 1 wyb, k2.

ROW 11 (RS): K4, turn.

ROW 12 (WS): Sl 1 wyb, k3.

ROW 13 (RS): K5, turn.

ROW 14 (WS): Sl 1 wyb, k4.

ROW 15 (RS): K6, turn.

ROW 16 (WS): Sl 1 wyb, k5.

ROWS 17–20: K7.

ROW 21 (RS): K6, turn.

ROW 22 (WS): Sl 1 wyb, k5.

ROW 23 (RS): K5, turn.

ROW 24 (WS): Sl 1 wyb, k4.

ROW 25 (RS): K4, turn.

ROW 26 (WS): Sl 1 wyb, k3.

ROW 27 (RS): K3, turn.

ROW 28 (WS): Sl 1 wyb, k2.

ROW 29 (RS): K2, turn.

ROW 30 (WS): Sl 1 wyb, k1.

ROWS 31–36: K7.

Work Rows 1–36 three more times.

Using extra needle, pick up and knit 7 sts along cast-on row. With RS facing RS and needles held parallel, work 3-needle bind-off across.

JOINING THE RINGS: Pick up and knit 6 sts along the straight section of the ring without short rows. Knit 4 rows.

Repeat on all sides where you wish to join the rings. Holding two rings RS facing RS and needles parallel, join with 3-needle bind off.

Shortened and Lengthened Rows #2

This pattern has no repeat. Just develop each shape as you knit. Knit all rows. So that you can learn the technique, I've written down the instructions for four of the shapes.

SHAPE 1

CO 14 sts.

Knit 9 rows.

BO 4 sts and knit rem sts.

Knit 1 row.

(BO 1 st, knit rem sts of row; knit 1 row) 3 times.

Knit 15 rows over rem sts.

BO.

SHAPE 2

Pick up and knit 9 sts centered on left side of Shape 1.

Knit 1 row.

Work short rows:

K2; turn.

Sl 1 wyf, k1.

K3; turn.

Sl 1 wyf, k2.

K4; turn.

Sl 1 wyf, k3.

K5; turn.

Sl 1 wyf, k4.

Knit 11 rows over all sts.

Work short rows and then even rows again.

Knit 5 rows.

CO 4 sts and knit rem sts across.

BO 3 sts and knit rem sts across.

Knit 7 rows.

BO.

SHAPE 3

Pick up and knit 7 sts under the 3-st bind-off on Shape 2.

Knit 9 rows.

Work short rows:

K4; turn

Sl 1 wyf, k3.

K5; turn.

Sl 1 wyf, k4.

K6; turn.

Sl 1 wyf, k5.

Knit 4 rows over all sts.

Work short rows:

K4; turn.

Sl 1 wyf, k3.

K5; turn.

Sl 1 wyf, k4.

K6; turn.

Sl 1 wyf, k5.

Knit 6 rows.

Work short rows and even rows again.

Knit 4 rows.

BO.

SHAPE 4

Pick up and knit 7 sts along outer bowed edge of Shape 3.

Knit 5 rows.

CO 10 sts and knit rem sts of row.

Knit 6 rows.

(K2tog at beginning of the row on left side of shape) 4 times.

BO 5 sts and knit rem sts of row.

(K2tog at beginning of the row on left side of shape) 3 times.

CO 3 sts and knit rem sts of row.

K2tog at beginning of the row on left side of shape until no stitches remain.

TECHNIQUES & ABBREVIATIONS

ABBREVIATIONS

BO	bind off
cm	centimeter(s)
CO	cast on
dec	decrease
dpn	double-pointed needles
inc	increase
k	knit
K-CO	Knit cast-on = knit 1 st, leaving old st on left needle, twist the new stitch and place on left needle; rep from.
k1f&b	knit into front and then back of same stitch
k2tog	knit 2 together
p	purl
p2tog	purl 2 together

RS	right side
psso	pass slipped stitch over
rem	remain, remaining
rnd(s)	round(s)
sl	slip
st(s)	stitch(es)
tbl	through back loop(s)
WS	wrong side
wyb	with yarn back (in back of work)
wyf	with yarn forward (at front of work)

Pattern repeats are indicated by asterisks (*). The asterisk indicates the start of the instruction to be repeated.

KNITTING WITH BEADS

A number of decades after its previous popularity, the tradition of knitting with beads has recently been revived. Mostly knitters have made beaded wrist warmers. I realized that sweaters could be beautifully embellished with beads and that the beads could be combined with simple surface patterns. To knit with beads, you first have to string the beads onto the yarn. Beads are positioned on the wrong side. The beads are placed between two stitches and, since the yarn strand lies on the right side, the beads also lie on the right side. So that the beads don't slide out of position, they have to be bordered with purl stitches, as seen from the right side.

OPPOSITE PAGE, TOP LEFT: On a stockinette stitch fabric, work one row of reverse stockinette, adding beads to every stitch.

OPPOSITE PAGE, TOP RIGHT: Place a number of beads close together to create shapes on the fabric. On garter stitch, the beads complement the texture of the fabric, and the emphasis is on the color difference.

OPPOSITE PAGE, MIDDLE LEFT: Place beads in the middle of patches of reverse stockinette on a stockinette background to further make them stand out.

OPPOSITE PAGE, MIDDLE RIGHT: Place single beads at regular spacing to create a polka dot effect.

OPPOSITE PAGE, BOTTOM LEFT: Contrasting color beads outline a shape on a stockinette stitch fabric.

OPPOSITE PAGE, BOTTOM RIGHT: Use multiple colors of beads and place them against larger patches of contrasting fabric.

For a different way to create texture and color, thread beads onto your yarn and add them into your fabric as you are working. After working a stitch, pull the bead up close to your needle so that it becomes trapped on the fabric between stitches.

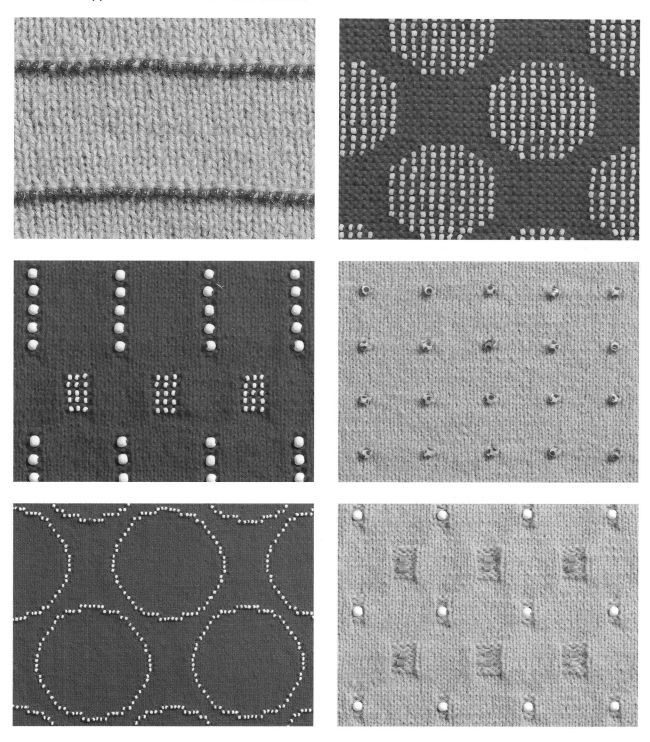

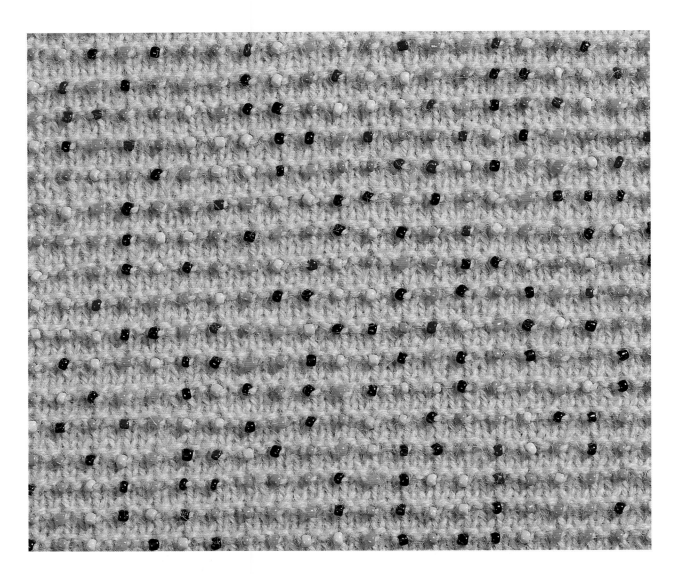

An almost tweed-like look can be created by placing
a large number of beads in a variety of colors close
together in a regular pattern. In this swatch, the beads
are worked into a row of reverse stockinette on a stockinette stitch fabric.

Placing beads on simple fabrics can create very sophisticated looks.

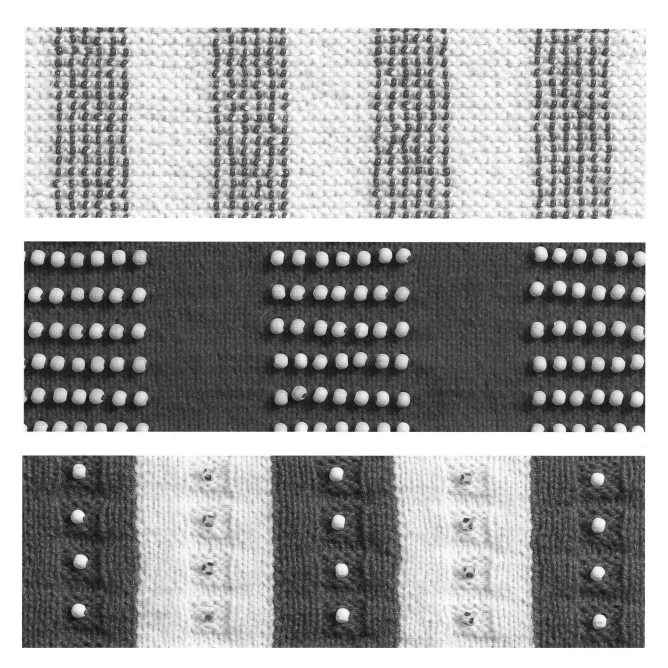

TOP: Create groups of vertical lines on garter stitch to create a contrast with the horizontal lines of the fabric.

MIDDLE: Add groups of larger beads in horizontal lines on a stockinette stitch fabric to contrast with the vertical lines of the fabric.

BOTTOM: Use multiple colors of yarn and multiple colors of beads to create contrast.

Any of the patterns in the book can be further enhanced with beads. Experiment!

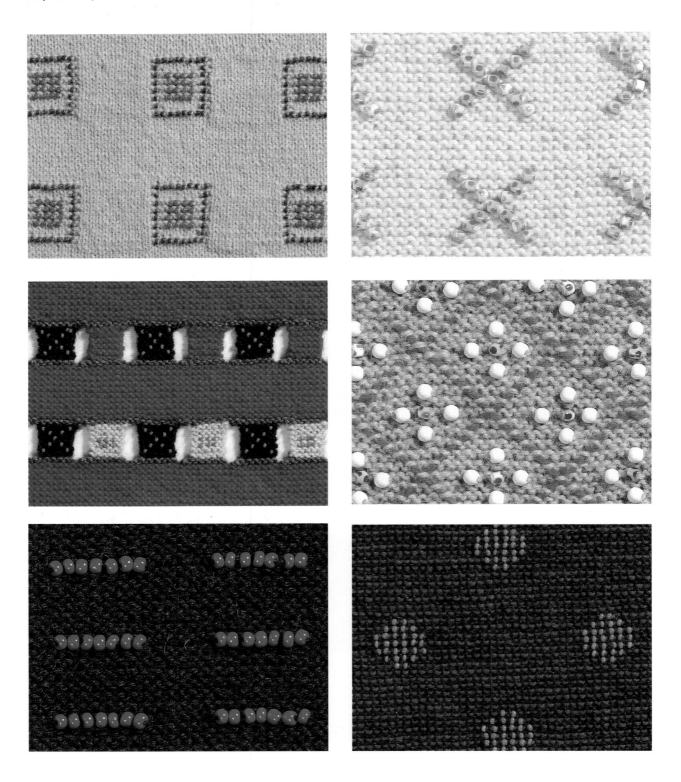

INTARSIA

Each section of the pattern is worked with a separate strand of yarn. When changing colors, bring the old working yarn over the yarn to be used in the next section. Always twist yarns on the wrong side of the fabric.

KNITTED CAST-ON (K-CO)

If there is no stitch to begin working the knitted cast-on into, make a slipknot loop to begin. Knit 1 stitch, leaving the loop or old stitch on the left needle. Twist the new stitch and place on left needle. The stitches sit on the needle so that the next row is easy to work.

ONE-ROW BUTTONHOLES

1. Bring yarn in front and slip 1 st.

2. Take yarn to back and slip 1 st.

3. BO the first slipped st over the second.

4. Continue to slip 1 st and then BO 1 until buttonhole is desired width. The yarn does not follow across these sts.

5. Slip the last st back to left needle.

6. Turn work.

7. Hold yarn behind work.

8. CO the same number of sts as bound off + 1. (Cast on by inserting the right needle between the nearest 2 sts on left needle, yarn around needle and through. At the same time, twist the stitch as it is placed on the left needle. Now the sts sit on the needle so it will be easy to knit the next row.)

9. Repeat the cast-on by inserting right needle between the 2 sts nearest tip of left needle, etc.

10. Place the yarn between the needle tips and in front of the knitting before the last st and the extra cast-on st are placed on the needle.

11. Turn work.

12. Slip 1 st from left to right needle.

13. BO the extra cast-on st over the slipped one.

CALCULATIONS FOR MAKING A KNITTED GARMENT

1. Make a gauge swatch using the same yarn and technique as for the garment, including ribbing if there is any on the garment. The gauge swatch should measure about 4¾" × 4¾" (12 × 12 cm).

2. Count the number of stitches and rows in 4" (10 cm).

3. On a paper mock-up, measure out the width of the garment in inches (centimeters). Multiply by the number of stitches per inch (centimeter) (that is, the number of stitches per 4" (10 cm) divided by 4 (10).

4. After the ribbing on the cuff (if there is a cuff) of a sleeve, you should increase the total number of stitches. Take the difference between the number of stitches in the cuff and the number of stitches in the sleeve and divide that (the difference) by the number of stitches in the cuff. The result indicates how many stitches you should have between each increase.

5. Calculate the number of rows for the sleeve (above the cuff). Calculate the number of stitches at the top of the sleeve. The difference divided by 2 is the number of increases that should be made for the sleeve width on each side. Divide the number of rows by this figure and then you have the number of rows between increase rows. As you work, the sleeve can be compared with the paper model and you can make adjustments as necessary.

6. Measure how many stitches you need to bind off for the neck by placing the knitted piece against the paper model.

MEASUREMENT SCHEMATICS FOR KNITTED SWEATER OR CARDIGAN

Whenever I make a garment using my pattern motifs, I always begin with a full-size paper model. I use either craft or wrapping paper. Reuse of gift wrap is another alternative. Below I've described how to make a garment with a simple shape where the pattern is dominant. I haven't included the amount of ease or size of the neck because those are personal choices that also depend on current fashion. If I am not sure about the projected measurements, I measure a garment I have on hand and that fits me well. Other materials you'll need: measuring tape, pen, ruler, and scissors.

Sweater Front

1. Draw a center line on the paper. The piece of paper should be larger than the width of the garment.

2. At a right angle from the center line, draw the shoulder line (straight). You could also use the top edge of the paper as the shoulder line.

3. Draw the neckline freehand, making it a bit small (the width from the center line should be about 2½" (6 cm). After the paper model is complete with all the other measurements, you can shape the neck while standing in front of a mirror.

4. Measure from one point on the section between the neck and shoulder for the sweater's desired length and mark that on the model.

5. Measure the circumference of the sweater, adding in ease. Divide that measurement by 4 and mark the right angle from the center line up and down on the model. Join the points with a line.

6. Fold along the center line and cut out the model.

7. Hold the model against the body in front of a mirror and draw the rounded shape as desired for neckline. Inside the neckline, draw a line for placement of beginning of ribbing. Cut out neckline.

Sweater Back

The neckline is the only difference between the front and back of sweater.

8. Draw a center line, on a smaller piece of paper and mark out width of back and neck, making sure neck is same width as on front. Make a shallow rounded shape about ¾" (2 cm) deep for back neck. Cut out the model and shape the back neck as for front.

Sweater Sleeves

9. Draw a center line on a new piece of paper.

10. At a right angle on one side of the center line draw a line for the top of the sleeve (or use the top edge of the paper for this line).

11. Measure, with arm slightly bent, the length of the sleeve from the point between the neck and shoulder to wrist. Decrease by the measurement for the shoulder. Mark the length on the paper model.

12. Measure the circumference for the cuff and width of the sleeve above the cuff, taking into consideration the circumference at the elbow as well as at top of arm. Divide the three measurements by 2 and mark them at a right angle from the center line. Draw joining lines between the measurements.

13. Fold along center line and cut out model.

Cardigan

14. Set up as for sweater front. Draw a line ⅝" (1.5 cm) to the right of the center line and mark the placement of the buttonholes down this line. Make the paper model for the other side of the front mirror image. The back and sleeves are the same as for the sweater.

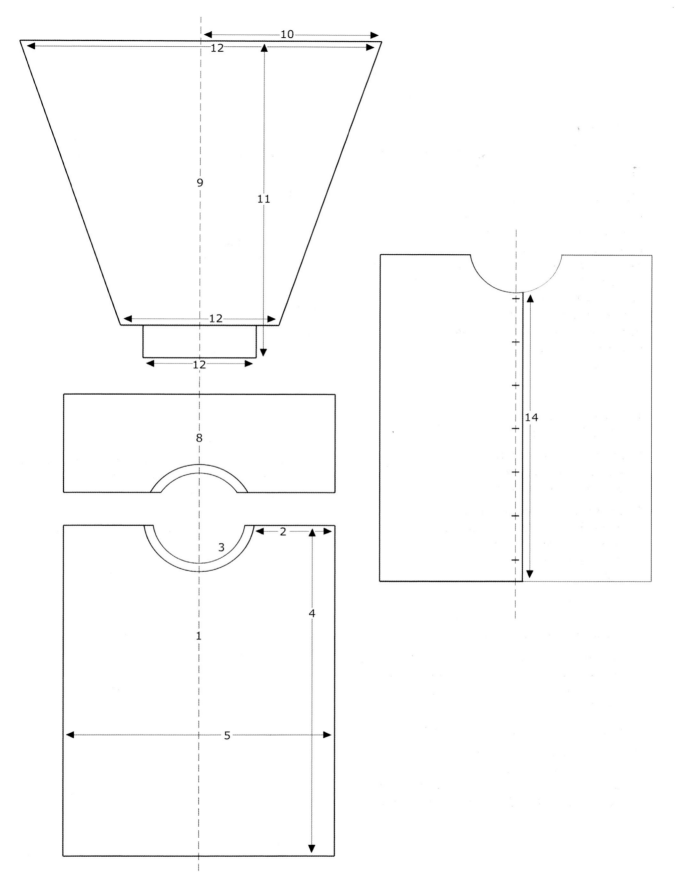

About
BRITT-MARIE CHRISTOFFERSSON

ANNELI PALMSKÖLD

Britt-Marie Christoffersson's name appears in most of the accounts of Swedish textile design during the 1960s and 1970s. Less often mentioned, though, are her inroads into handknitting. But anyone interested in learning about knitting would be well served by learning more about Britt-Marie Christoffersson. Her contributions to renewing and developing the techniques of knitting are substantial.

Britt-Marie's unique vision is visible in the surface textures, colors, and proportions she chooses. Her signature as designer is obsessive and intense work with the technical aspects of knitting, expressed in multiple slight variations of a theme.

FROM BORÅS TO STOCKHOLM

Britt-Marie Christoffersson began her life in Borås, Sweden. To grow up in Borås during the 1940s and 1950s was to grow up in a city dominated by textile factories. The city was known for its main industry and display windows everywhere were packed with textiles in various patterns and colors. Britt-Marie was inspired to apply to the Textile Institute in Borås where she was enrolled in the two-year program from 1957–59, with a focus on industrial textile production. The program of work included weaving and pattern drawing.

Sources of inspiration in Borås ranged from the exhibits in the art galleries to a particular type of patterning that Britt-Marie calls "un-designed." To get an idea of what these look like, imagine simple small patterns in the shape of stripes, blocks, triangles, and dots. The fascination with un-designed shapes is

expressed in variations of the motifs that Britt-Marie Christoffersson now calls "apron" patterns.

Her studies at Textile Institute in Borås were followed by the four-year program at the Konstfack (University College of Arts, Crafts, and Design) in Stockholm from 1959–1962. With the strong foundation of her training at Borås, Britt-Marie was able to move directly into the second year of the program under the leadership of Edna Martin, the head teacher in the textile department. While at Konstfack, she formed friendships that would prove instrumental to her evolution. Britt-Marie's class included Birgitta Hahn, who was also a member and developer of what would later become known as the "10-Group," as well as Raine Navin, Kristina Torsson, Helena Henschen, and Veronica Nygren. Together they formed the textile company Mah-Jong. This generation of textile designers was soon to leave an indelible mark on modern Swedish textile design.

A CHANGING INDUSTRY

During the first few years after her education at Konstfack, Britt-Marie was employed in the textile industry, but she soon decided to freelance. By that time (the mid-1960s), designers began to criticize certain standards of the textile industry—namely those that usually prevented a designer from participating in the complete process from concept to finished product. Textile companies bought the pattern ideas from designers and would end up producing certain patterns, but not others. "Sometimes you didn't even recognize your own designs on the store shelves," Britt-Marie says. This situation ultimately led to the formation of the 10-Group, in which the designers became colleagues who controlled the entire process of textile development, from pattern to fabric.

Another concern of the 10-Group was a questioning of consumer society and overproduction of material within a capitalist system. By offering basic products with complementary patterns, the 10-Group did their part to stem the overflow. The group had ten participants and ten fabrics. Each of the designers worked in her or his own way to express the designs. The fabrics could be combined and were printed in a complementary color scale. However, the collections proved to be difficult to distribute to marketers. Ultimately the group was forced to open its own shop.

Britt-Marie Christoffersson's pattern contributions often came in the form of stripes. She characterizes her patterns sold under the 10-Group's label as "stripes, geometric, and simple." "Those were sixteen extremely educative and rich years. I couldn't work as I do now if I hadn't been with the 10-Group," she says.

A DEDICATION TO KNITTING

Britt-Marie left the group in 1986 to concentrate on knitting. Her interest in knitting was awakened during a general revival of the craft that began around 1978. "I decided that now I should study knitting as thoroughly as I had studied weaving while in college," she says. "The technique certainly warrants it, so why hadn't we dedicated ourselves to it at school?"

The project of learning as much as possible about the techniques of knitting led to a systematic and organized production of swatches. Her reference sources were pattern books in Swedish and English. These studies resulted in her creating more than 1,000 swatches in various formats. One way of developing her knowledge was to learn more about Swedish knitting traditions. Inspired by her training at Konstfack, where researching old textile techniques was an obvious path for learning, Britt-Marie began inventorying knitted textiles in Swedish museums. She transcribed about a hundred patterns, which became the foundation for the selections presented in her book, *Swedish Sweaters: New Designs from Historical Examples* (Newtown,

Connecticut: Taunton, 1990; original Swedish edition published in 1988). Many of the samples traveled in an exhibition "Old Patterns, New Sweaters, Worldwide Knitting Techniques." The exhibit included garments designed by Britt-Marie Christoffersson and inspired by various sources in her inventorying. The exhibit attracted a large and positive response and was shown at thirty-three venues from December 1985 through February 1992. Alongside the exhibits, Britt-Marie taught workshops stemming from her own course materials.

At the end of the exhibit's tours, ("basic training in knitting," as Britt-Marie Christoffersson calls the project), she began the work on the next exhibition. It was eventually called "Knitting: A Handwork to Develop," to point out that the techniques of knitting constantly change and evolve. By February 2009, that exhibit had been displayed in a dozen places, from Denmark, to Japan, and beyond. As with her previous exhibit, Britt-Marie teaches workshops in conjunction with the exhibit. Now she is hard at work on a third exhibit, which has the theme "Embroidery on Knitting." At the same time, Britt-Marie Christoffersson engages deeply with her courses, always learning from her workshop students. By constantly maintaining a dialogue about the patterns, she can continue to improve and develop them.

"It should be a pleasure for my eyes."

Britt-Marie Christoffersson says that her focus is on color, form, and building patterns by coordinating shapes, colors, and surfaces. Her goal is that the pieces "should be a pleasure for my eyes."

So why did she choose knitting? What was it like to go from producing pattern designs for industry and, via the 10-Group's comprehensive production, to handknitting? "I always wanted to make things with my hands. It is pleasing to create structures instead of printing flat patterns," Britt-Marie Christoffersson says. She continues, saying that, with knitting, she can work out her ideas rather quickly and have a visible result in the form of a swatch. Compared with the long process from concept to product as in the textile industry, it's an advantage. But the word "quick" is relative. It might

JARI VÄLITALO

take one or two days to make a swatch depending on how complicated the pattern is. In addition, Britt-Marie likes both knitting and embroidery because, she says, she is a bit lazy. "It is so handy to work with fine needles and yarn," she says. "It's comfortable and I can quickly move from concept to product. It is a free technique. The same applies to embroidery. I can sit in a corner and be independent."

Anyone who knits knows that the ways we knit varies; some knit tightly and some knit loosely. This, of course, affects the end result and means not only that the size of the garment can change, but that the patterns and surface textures will look different. Britt-Marie Christoffersson knits firmly, tightly, and perfectly evenly. Because she considers color the most important

factor, the type of yarn she knits with plays a lesser role although her basic material is wool yarn. "I knit only with wool for the most part," she says "I like its warmth in my hands. It is easy and lovely to knit with."

The most obvious feature of Britt-Marie Christoffersson's design work is her way of using and blending colors. She loves colors and employs them freely in her own personal color combinations. "I use colors that no one would want to wear," she says. A professional designer can be overly self critical and Britt-Marie Christoffersson is far from always satisfied with her results. She frequently sorts through her pieces and throws away any that didn't work out and are failures in her view: "It bothers me to have them lying about."

FOR FURTHER READING

CHRISTOFFERSSON, BRITT-MARIE. *SWEDISH SWEATERS: NEW DESIGNS FROM HISTORICAL EXAMPLES*. TRANS. GUNNEL MELCHERS. NEWTOWN, CONNECTICUT: TAUNTON, 1990.

RUTT, RICHARD. *A HISTORY OF HAND KNITTING*. LOVELAND, COLORADO: INTERWEAVE, 2003.

This book is regarded as one of the best and most detailed on the subject.

THOMAS, MARY. *MARY THOMAS'S KNITTING BOOK*. MINEOLA, NEW YORK: DOVER PUBLICATIONS, 1972.

_____. *MARY THOMAS'S BOOK OF KNITTING PATTERNS*. MINEOLA, NEW YORK: DOVER PUBLICATIONS, 1972.

These books were originally published in 1938 and 1943 respectively. Both of Mary Thomas's books offer amusing, basic, and informative reading, particularly for anyone who also knits.

INDEX

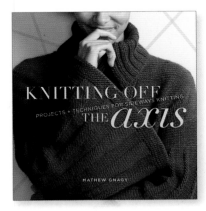